EDITOR: Maryanne Blacker

FOOD EDITOR: Pamela Clark

■ ■ ■

DESIGNER: Paula Wooller

■ ■ ■

DEPUTY FOOD EDITOR: Jan Castorina

ASSISTANT FOOD EDITOR: Kathy Snowball

ASSOCIATE FOOD EDITOR: Enid Morrison

SENIOR HOME ECONOMISTS: Jill Lange, Louise Patniotis, Kathy Wharton

HOME ECONOMISTS: Tracey Kern, Alexandra McCowan, Kathy McGarry, Andrew Nunn, Maggie Quickenden, Dimitra Stais

EDITORIAL COORDINATOR: Elizabeth Hooper

KITCHEN ASSISTANT: Amy Wong

■ ■ ■

STYLISTS: Marie-Helene Clauzon, Rosemary de Santis, Carolyn Fienberg, Jane Hann, Lisa Hilton, Jacqui Hing

PHOTOGRAPHERS: Kevin Brown, Robert Clark, Robert Taylor, Jon Waddy

■ ■ ■

HOME LIBRARY STAFF

ASSISTANT EDITOR: Judy Newman

DESIGNER: Robbylee Phelan

EDITORIAL COORDINATOR: Lara Quinlin

■ ■ ■

ACP PUBLISHER: Richard Walsh

ACP ASSOCIATE PUBLISHER: Bob Neil

■ ■ ■

Produced by The Australian Women's Weekly Home Library. Typeset by Letter Perfect, Sydney. Printed by Dai Nippon Co., Ltd in Japan. Published by Australian Consolidated Press, 54 Park Street Sydney.
◆ AUSTRALIA: Distributed by Network Distribution Company, 54 Park Street Sydney, (02) 282 8777.
◆ NEW ZEALAND: Distributed in New Zealand by Netlink Distribution Company, 17B Hargreaves St, Level 5, College Hill, Auckland 1, (9) 302 7616.
◆ UNITED KINGDOM: Distributed in the U.K. by Australian Consolidated Press (UK) Ltd, 20 Galowhill Rd, Brackmills, Northampton NN4 OOE, (0604) 760 456.
◆ CANADA: Distributed in Canada by Whitecap Books Ltd, 1086 West 3rd St, North Vancouver V7P 3J6, (604) 9809852.
◆ SOUTH AFRICA: Distributed in South Africa by Intermag, PO Box 57394, Springfield 2137, (011) 4933200. ACN 000 031 747.

■ ■ ■

Cooking for Two

Includes index.
ISBN 0 949128 88 0.

1. Cookery for Two. (Series : Australian Women's Weekly Home Library).

641.561

■ ■ ■

© A C P 1992
This publication is copyright. No part of it may be reproduced or transmitted in any form without the written permission of the publishers.

■ ■ ■

COVER: Salmon with Spinach and Lime Butter Sauce and Peppered Potatoes, page 61
OPPOSITE: Sake Duck with Snow Peas and Avocado, page 9
BACK COVER: Poached Fruit with Mascarpone Cheese, page 121.

COOK FOR TWO

The time-saving bonus in this book is that each main course has its own accompaniments, so you know at a glance exactly what to serve. It's a terrific help when planning, because you can quickly suit all occasions from formal to casual, perhaps a candlelit dinner for two, a quick snack before the theatre or a simple home meal. But it's more than a book for two. If you're on your own, you'd have enough for two servings, or could halve the recipes. The recipes can be doubled to serve four or further increased for entertaining.

Pamela Clark

FOOD EDITOR

BRITISH & NORTH AMERICAN READERS: Please note that Australian cup and spoon measurements are metric. Conversion charts for cup and spoon measurements and oven temperatures appear on page 127.
A glossary explaining unfamiliar terms and ingredients appears on page 124.

STARTERS & SNACKS

Perfectly proportioned yet generous recipes for two are reasonably simple so you won't be

cooking for hours! There are hot and cold soups, plus starters ranging widely from elegant

duck, beetroot ravioli, and eggplant and pepper timbales, to super-easy

platters of ingredients you can pick up from the delicatessen on the way home. Tasty

snacks include mini pocket pizzas and roast potatoes, both with terrific toppings.

SPICY COCONUT SOUP

50g dried Japanese noodles
1 tablespoon oil
1 onion, chopped
1 clove garlic, crushed
½ teaspoon ground cumin
½ teaspoon turmeric
½ teaspoon ground coriander
1 teaspoon curry powder
2 cups chicken stock
180ml can coconut cream
70g small cooked shelled prawns
100g white fish fillets, sliced
8 leaves English spinach, shredded

Add noodles to pan of boiling water, boil, uncovered, until just tender; drain. Divide noodles between 2 serving bowls.

Heat oil in pan, add onion and garlic, cook, stirring, until onion is soft. Add spices, cook, stirring, until aromatic. Stir in stock and coconut cream, bring to boil. Stir in prawns, fish and spinach, simmer, uncovered, until soup is heated through and fish is just tender. Pour soup over noodles in bowls.

■ Recipe best made just before serving.
■ Freeze: Not suitable.
■ Microwave: Suitable.

RIGHT: Spicy Coconut Soup.

China from Christofle.

POTATO AND LEEK SOUP WITH CRISPY BACON

2 large (about 400g) potatoes
4 bacon rashers
2 tablespoons oil
1 small leek, sliced
1 clove garlic, crushed
2½ cups chicken stock
⅓ cup cream
¼ cup milk
1 tablespoon chopped fresh chives
1 teaspoon French mustard

Chop potatoes into 1cm cubes. Cut bacon into thin strips. Heat half the oil in pan, add bacon, cook, stirring, until bacon is crisp; drain on absorbent paper.

Heat remaining oil in pan, add leek and garlic, cook, stirring, until leek is soft. Stir in stock and half the potatoes, simmer, covered, until potato is tender. Blend or process potato mixture until smooth; return to pan with remaining potato and half the bacon, simmer, uncovered, until potato is tender. Stir in cream, milk, chives and mustard, stir until heated through. Serve soup sprinkled with remaining bacon.

■ Soup can be made a day ahead.
■ Storage: Covered, in refrigerator.
■ Freeze: Not suitable.
■ Microwave: Suitable.

PUMPKIN AND BEAN SOUP

2 cups water
2 tablespoons dried haricot beans
¼ red pepper
4 chives
20g butter
1 small onion, chopped
1 clove garlic, crushed
½ teaspoon curry powder
250g pumpkin, peeled, chopped
2 cups chicken stock
¼ cup grated smoked cheese
1 tablespoon sour cream

Combine water and beans in bowl, cover, stand overnight.

Transfer undrained beans to pan, simmer, covered, about 1 hour or until beans are tender; drain.

Cut pepper into thin strips, cut chives into 6cm lengths. Heat butter in pan, add onion, garlic and curry powder, cook, stirring, until onion is soft. Add pumpkin and stock, simmer, covered, until pumpkin is soft. Blend or process pumpkin mixture until smooth.

Return pumpkin mixture to pan, stir in beans and pepper, bring to boil. Add cheese and cream, stir until heated through. Serve soup topped with chives.

■ Recipe can be made a day ahead.
■ Storage: Covered, in refrigerator.
■ Freeze: Suitable.
■ Microwave: Suitable.

TOMATO AND RED PEPPER SOUP WITH PESTO

1 red pepper
20g butter
1 small red Spanish onion, chopped
1 stick celery, chopped
1 small carrot, chopped
2 large (about 500g) tomatoes, peeled, seeded, chopped
2 cups chicken stock

PESTO
½ cup fresh basil leaves
1 tablespoon pine nuts, toasted
1 clove garlic, crushed
1 tablespoon grated parmesan cheese
¼ cup olive oil

Quarter pepper, remove seeds and membrane. Grill pepper skin side up until skin blisters and blackens. Peel skin, cut pepper into strips.

Heat butter in pan, add onion, celery and carrot, cook, stirring, until onion is soft. Add pepper, tomatoes and stock, simmer, covered, 15 minutes; cool.

Blend or process mixture until smooth. Cover, refrigerate until cold. Serve soup topped with pesto.
Pesto: Blend or process all ingredients until smooth.

- Recipe can be made a day ahead.
- Storage: Covered, in refrigerator.
- Freeze: Pesto suitable.
- Microwave: Suitable.

BROCCOLI SOUP WITH CHEESY WONTONS

300g broccoli
15g butter
1 small onion, chopped
½ teaspoon ground cumin
2 cups chicken stock
1 bay leaf
1 tablespoon cream

CHEESY WONTONS
¼ cup grated Swiss cheese
2 teaspoons chopped fresh parsley
1 teaspoon sesame seeds
8 square wonton wrappers
egg white
oil for deep-frying

Reserve 12 small broccoli flowerets, chop remaining broccoli. Boil, steam or microwave broccoli flowerets until just tender; drain.

Heat butter in pan, add onion and cumin, cook, stirring, until onion is soft. Add chopped broccoli, stock and bay leaf to onion mixture, simmer, covered, until broccoli is just tender, discard bay leaf. Blend or process mixture until smooth, stir in cream and reserved flowerets. Serve with cheesy wontons.
Cheesy Wontons: Combine cheese, parsley and seeds in bowl. Brush edges of wonton wrappers with a little egg white, divide cheese mixture evenly between wonton wrappers, roll up to enclose filling. Press ends together firmly with fork. Deep-fry wontons in hot oil until lightly browned, drain on absorbent paper.

- Soup can be made a day ahead.
- Storage: Covered, in refrigerator.
- Freeze: Soup and uncooked wontons suitable.
- Microwave: Soup suitable.

LEFT: From left: Pumpkin and Bean Soup, Potato and Leek Soup with Crispy Bacon.
BELOW: From left: Tomato and Red Pepper Soup with Pesto, Broccoli Soup with Cheesy Wontons.

CHILLED CHERVIL AND LETTUCE SOUP

20g butter
1 small leek, chopped
1 small potato, chopped
3 cups chicken stock
⅓ cup frozen peas
2 tablespoons chopped fresh chervil
½ small lettuce, chopped
4 leaves English spinach, chopped
2 teaspoons lemon juice
½ cup cream

Heat butter in pan, add leek, cook, stirring, until soft. Stir in potato, stock and peas, simmer, covered, until potato is tender. Add chervil, lettuce and spinach, simmer further 2 minutes; cool. Blend or process soup until smooth. Transfer soup to bowl, stir in juice and cream; cover, refrigerate until cold. Serve soup with extra chervil leaves and chives, if desired.

- Recipe can be made a day ahead.
- Storage: Covered, in refrigerator.
- Freeze: Not suitable.
- Microwave: Suitable.

CARROT PARSNIP SOUP WITH RYE CROUTONS

15g butter
2 medium (about 200g) carrots, finely chopped
2 medium (about 200g) parsnips, finely chopped
1 medium (about 150g) potato, finely chopped
2 tablespoons dry white wine
3 cups vegetable stock

RYE CROUTONS
2 thin slices rye bread
15g butter, melted
½ teaspoon ground cumin

Heat butter in pan, add vegetables and wine, simmer, covered, stirring occasionally, until vegetables are just tender. Add stock, simmer, uncovered, 10 minutes.

Blend or process mixture until smooth, return to pan, stir until heated through. Serve soup with rye croutons. Top with dill sprigs, if desired.

Rye Croutons: Cut bread into 3½cm rounds. Brush with combined butter and cumin. Cook croutons in heated pan until crisp; drain on absorbent paper.

- Soup and croutons can be made a day ahead.
- Storage: Soup, covered, in refrigerator. Croutons in airtight container.
- Freeze: Soup suitable.
- Microwave: Soup suitable.

ABOVE: From top: Carrot Parsnip Soup with Rye Croutons, Chilled Chervil and Lettuce Soup.

China from Christofle.

BEETROOT RAVIOLI WITH CRISPY BASIL

20g butter
1 clove garlic, crushed
1 medium (about 200g) beetroot,
**   peeled, finely grated**
½ onion, chopped
2 tablespoons grated parmesan
**   cheese**
24 round gow gees pastry
50g butter, extra
⅓ cup shredded fresh basil

Heat butter in pan, add garlic, beetroot and onion, cook, stirring, over low heat about 15 minutes or until beetroot is tender; cool.

Stir cheese into beetroot mixture.

Place 1 level teaspoon of beetroot mixture in centre of each pastry round, press mixture to flatten slightly. Lightly brush edges of pastry with water, fold pastry to enclose filling, press edges together to seal. Add ravioli to pan of boiling water, simmer, uncovered, about 5 minutes or until ravioli are tender; drain.

Heat extra butter in pan, add basil, cook, stirring, until basil is crisp. Remove basil from pan; drain on absorbent paper. Add ravioli to same pan, gently stir until well coated in butter. Spoon ravioli onto 2 serving dishes, top with crispy basil.

■ Ravioli can be made a day ahead.
■ Storage: Covered, in refrigerator.
■ Freeze: Uncooked ravioli suitable.
■ Microwave: Suitable.

BELOW: Beetroot Ravioli with Crispy Basil.

EGGPLANT AND PEPPER TIMBALES

½ green pepper
½ yellow pepper
½ red pepper
½ medium (about 150g) eggplant
2 tablespoons olive oil
30g butter
1 small red Spanish onion, finely chopped
1 clove garlic, crushed
1 medium (about 130g) tomato, peeled, seeded, chopped

TOMATO COULIS
1 large (about 250g) tomato, peeled, seeded, chopped
1 teaspoon tarragon wine vinegar
3 teaspoons olive oil
1 clove garlic, crushed
1 teaspoon chopped fresh basil
1 teaspoon chopped fresh chives

Lightly grease 2 timbale moulds (1 cup capacity), line with plastic wrap.

Remove seeds and membrane from peppers. Grill peppers skin side up until skin blisters and blackens. Peel away skin, chop peppers. Peel eggplant, cut eggplant into 1cm cubes. Heat oil in pan, add eggplant, cook until lightly browned, drain on absorbent paper.

Heat butter in same pan, add peppers, onion and garlic, cook, stirring, until onion is soft. Stir in tomato, remove from heat, stir in eggplant.

Spoon mixture into prepared timbales; press down firmly. Cover with foil, place in baking dish, add enough boiling water to come half way up sides of timbales. Bake in moderate oven 45 minutes, remove from baking dish; cool. Refrigerate

timbales 3 hours or overnight. Turn timbales out, serve with tomato coulis.

Tomato Coulis: Combine all ingredients in bowl; mix well. Cover, stand 1 hour before serving.

■ Recipe can be made a day ahead.
■ Storage: Covered, in refrigerator.
■ Freeze: Not suitable.
■ Microwave: Suitable.

SAKE DUCK WITH SNOW PEAS AND AVOCADO

100g snow peas
½ red pepper, thinly sliced
1 tablespoon oil
1 (about 200g) single duck breast fillet
¼ cup sake
2 tablespoons light soy sauce
1 tablespoon brown sugar
1 tablespoon rice vinegar
½ small avocado, chopped

Boil, steam or microwave peas and pepper until just tender; drain, rinse under cold water, pat dry with absorbent paper.

Heat oil in pan, add duck, cook skin side down until skin is well browned and crisp. Turn duck, cook on other side for about 5 minutes or until duck is just tender. Remove duck from pan, stand 10 minutes before slicing thinly.

Combine sake, sauce, sugar and vinegar in clean pan, simmer, uncovered, about 2 minutes or until sauce is thick and syrupy. Remove from heat, add duck; coat well. Serve duck warm with snow peas, pepper and avocado.

■ Recipe best made just before serving.
■ Freeze: Not suitable.
■ Microwave: Snow peas and pepper suitable.

LEFT: Eggplant and Pepper Timbales.
ABOVE: Sake Duck with Snow Peas and Avocado.

Left: Plates, glasses and cutlery from The Bay Tree Kitchen Shop; pepper grinder and Alessi metal basket from Remo. Above: Plate from Amy's Tableware.

AVOCADO AND GOATS' CHEESE SALAD

1 large (about 250g) tomato, peeled, seeded, chopped
¼ red pepper, chopped
1 small red Spanish onion, chopped
2 tablespoons red wine vinegar
¼ cup olive oil
1 tablespoon chopped fresh basil
1 small French bread stick
20g butter, melted
50g goats' cheese, crumbled
½ avocado, sliced
1 teaspoon chopped fresh basil, extra

Combine tomato, pepper, onion, vinegar, oil and basil in bowl, cover, stand 2 hours.

Slice bread diagonally into 4 x 2cm rounds, reserve remaining bread for another dish. Brush each side of slices with butter, place on oven tray. Bake in moderate oven about 10 minutes, turning once, or until crisp.

Drain tomato mixture, reserve juice. Place 2 croutes on each serving plate, top with tomato mixture and cheese. Serve with avocado, drizzled with reserved juice; sprinkle with extra basil.

- Tomato mixture can be prepared 2 hours ahead. Croutes best assembled just before serving.
- Storage: Tomato mixture, covered, in refrigerator.
- Freeze: Not suitable.
- Microwave: Not suitable.

OYSTERS WITH SHALLOTS AND BALSAMIC DRESSING

1 green shallot
12 fresh oysters in half shells

BALSAMIC DRESSING
2 teaspoons balsamic vinegar
3 teaspoons olive oil
¼ teaspoon cracked black peppercorns
½ teaspoon seeded mustard

Cut shallot into thin strips, then into 3cm lengths. Place oysters on serving plates, top with shallot strips, sprinkle with balsamic dressing.

Balsamic Dressing: Combine all ingredients in jar; shake well.

- Balsamic dressing can be made a day ahead.
- Storage: Covered, in refrigerator.
- Freeze: Not suitable.

LEFT: Top and front: Oysters with Shallots and Balsamic Dressing; centre: Avocado and Goats' Cheese Salad.
BELOW: Prosciutto Salad with Anchovy Dressing.

Left: Plates, cutlery and dressing container from The Bay Tree; pepper grinder from Remo; serviettes from Made Where.

PROSCIUTTO SALAD WITH ANCHOVY DRESSING

40g piece parmesan cheese
4 oak leaf lettuce leaves
4 cos lettuce leaves
60g sliced prosciutto
½ avocado, chopped
4 cherry tomatoes, halved
8 watercress sprigs

ANCHOVY DRESSING
¼ cup cream
2 teaspoons mayonnaise
4 drained anchovy fillets
1 soft-boiled egg

GARLIC CROUTONS
2 slices white bread
20g butter, melted
1 clove garlic, crushed

Using a vegetable peeler, slice cheese into shavings.

Arrange torn lettuce leaves, prosciutto, avocado, tomatoes and watercress on serving plates, top with anchovy dressing, sprinkle with garlic croutons and cheese.

Anchovy Dressing: Blend or process all ingredients until smooth.

Garlic Croutons: Remove crusts from bread, cut bread into 2cm cubes. Combine butter and garlic in small bowl, toss in bread cubes to coat. Place croutons on oven tray. Bake in moderately hot oven about 12 minutes or until lightly browned and crisp.

- Recipe best made just before serving.
- Freeze: Not suitable.
- Microwave: Not suitable.

SPICY CHICKEN WINGS WITH WATERCRESS SALAD

¼ cup oil
pinch cayenne pepper
2 teaspoons seasoned pepper
2 cloves garlic, crushed
1 teaspoon celery salt
1 onion, finely chopped
1 tablespoon chopped fresh thyme
3 teaspoons paprika
4 chicken wings

WATERCRESS SALAD
1 cup watercress sprigs
½ red pepper, sliced
2 tablespoons French dressing

Combine oil, peppers, garlic, salt, onion, thyme and paprika in bowl. Spread chicken with mixture, cover, refrigerate several hours or overnight.

Place chicken on wire rack in baking dish. Bake, uncovered, in moderately hot oven about 40 minutes or until chicken is tender. Serve with watercress salad.

Watercress Salad: Combine watercress, pepper and dressing in bowl; mix well.

■ Chicken can be prepared a day ahead. Watercress salad best prepared just before serving.
■ Storage: Covered, in refrigerator.
■ Freeze: Marinated chicken suitable.
■ Microwave: Not suitable.

TOMATO, OLIVE AND SQUID RISOTTO

2 large (about 500g) tomatoes,
    roughly chopped
1 tablespoon fresh rosemary leaves
1 tablespoon chopped fresh basil
1 bay leaf
2 cloves garlic, peeled
1 tablespoon tomato paste
1 tablespoon olive oil
1 small onion, chopped
2 cloves garlic, crushed, extra
2/3 cup arborio rice
2 tablespoons dry white wine
375g carton (1½ cups) fish stock
½ cup boiling water
100g squid hoods, sliced
8 black olives, halved
½ cup grated parmesan cheese

Combine tomatoes, herbs and garlic in small pan, cover, simmer about 20 minutes or until tomatoes are soft. Discard bay leaf, blend or process mixture until smooth; push through a sieve, stir in tomato paste.

Heat oil in pan, add onion, extra garlic and rice, cook, stirring, until onion is soft. Add wine, stir over heat until evaporated. Stir in ¼ cup of combined stock and water, cook, stirring, over very low heat until liquid is absorbed. Continue adding stock mixture very gradually, stirring until absorbed before next addition. Total cooking time should be about 25 minutes or until rice is tender.

Stir in tomato mixture, cook, stirring, until mixture is thickened. Add squid, cook, stirring, about 1 minute or until squid is tender. Stir in olives and cheese.

- Recipe best made just before serving.
- Freeze: Not suitable.
- Microwave: Suitable.

FISH BITELETS WITH RED PEPPER SAUCE

1 (about 450g) firm white fish cutlet
2 tablespoons oil
30g butter

RED PEPPER SAUCE
1 red pepper
½ teaspoon sugar
¼ cup cream

VEGETABLES
½ small leek
1 baby eggplant
¼ bunch fresh chives
2 tablespoons oil
1 teaspoon cracked black
    peppercorns

Cut fish into 3cm cubes. Heat oil and butter in pan, add fish, cook until lightly browned and just tender; drain on absorbent paper.

Spoon red pepper sauce onto serving plates, top with fish and vegetables.

Red Pepper Sauce: Quarter pepper, remove membrane and seeds. Place pepper on oven tray, skin side up, cook in moderately hot oven about 30 minutes or until skin is blackened and pepper is soft; cool. Remove skin from pepper; chop pepper. Blend or process pepper, sugar and cream until smooth, transfer mixture to pan, stir over heat until hot.

Vegetables: Using only white part of leek, cut leek and unpeeled eggplant into very fine strips about 9cm long. Cut chives into 9cm lengths. Heat oil in pan, add leek, eggplant, chives and pepper, cook, stirring, about 1 minute or until vegetables are just tender.

- Fish and vegetables best cooked just before serving. Red pepper sauce can be made a day ahead.
- Storage: Red pepper sauce, covered, in refrigerator.
- Freeze: Not suitable.
- Microwave: Vegetables suitable.

LEFT: From left: Spicy Chicken Wings with Watercress Salad, Tomato, Olive and Squid Risotto.
RIGHT: Fish Bitelets with Red Pepper Sauce.

Left: Plates from Made Where; cutlery from The Bay Tree; serviette and glasses from Lillywhites.

ASPARAGUS AND PASTA WITH SAFFRON CREAM

½ bunch (about 10 spears) thin fresh
   asparagus
100g tagliatelle pasta
20g butter
1 clove garlic, crushed
½ red pepper, sliced
1 small red Spanish onion, sliced
2 (about 120g) baby zucchini, sliced
300ml carton cream
3 saffron strands
10 leaves English spinach, shredded
1 tablespoon chopped fresh chives
freshly grated parmesan cheese

Cut asparagus into 4cm pieces. Add pasta to pan of boiling water, simmer, uncovered, until just tender; drain.

Heat butter in pan, add garlic, pepper, onion, zucchini and asparagus, stir-fry until vegetables are just tender, add cream, saffron and spinach. Bring to boil, simmer, stirring, until sauce is slightly thickened, stir in chives. Serve sauce over pasta, sprinkle with cheese.

■ Recipe best made just before serving.
■ Freeze: Not suitable.
■ Microwave: Suitable.

MUSSELS IN BLACK BEAN SAUCE

750g small mussels
1 cup water
2 tablespoons black bean sauce
4 medium (about 500g) tomatoes,
   peeled, seeded, chopped
2 teaspoons chopped fresh basil

To clean mussels, pull away beard. Use a stiff brush to scrub mussels under cold water. Soak mussels in several changes of cold water to remove any sand.

Combine water and sauce in large pan, bring to boil, add mussels, simmer, covered, about 3 minutes or until shells

have opened. Remove mussels immediately with slotted spoon. Bring liquid in pan to boil, add tomatoes, boil, uncovered, about 5 minutes or until sauce is thickened slightly. Return mussels to pan, stir until heated through. Serve mussels sprinkled with basil.

- Recipe best made just before serving.
- Freeze: Not suitable.
- Microwave: Suitable.

SPINACH AND MUSHROOM TARTLETS

⅔ cup plain flour
50g butter
2 teaspoons sesame seeds, toasted
1 egg yolk
1 tablespoon water, approximately

SPINACH FILLING
15g butter
1 green shallot, chopped
½ bunch (20 leaves) English spinach
pinch nutmeg
2 teaspoons light soy sauce

MUSHROOM FILLING
15g butter
1 clove garlic, crushed
100g oyster mushrooms

Grease 2 x 10cm flan tins. Sift flour into bowl, rub in butter, stir in seeds. Add yolk and enough water to make ingredients cling together. Press dough into ball, knead gently on floured surface until smooth; cover, refrigerate 30 minutes.

Cut pastry in half, roll each half on floured surface large enough to line prepared tins. Lift pastry into tins, trim edges, place on oven tray. Line pastry with paper, fill with dried beans or rice. Bake in moderately hot oven 10 minutes, remove paper and beans, bake further 10 minutes or until pastry is lightly browned. Spoon spinach and mushroom fillings into pastry cases just before serving.

Spinach Filling: Heat butter in pan, add shallot, spinach, nutmeg and sauce, cook, stirring, until spinach is soft.

Mushroom Filling: Heat butter in pan, add garlic and mushrooms, cook, stirring, until mushrooms are tender.

- Spinach filling and mushroom filling best made just before serving. Pastry cases can be made 2 days ahead.
- Storage: Pastry cases in airtight container.
- Freeze: Not suitable.
- Microwave: Fillings suitable.

LEFT: From back: Mussels in Black Bean Sauce, Asparagus and Pasta with Saffron Cream.
RIGHT: Spinach and Mushroom Tartlets.

Left: Plates, glasses, black and white cloth and serviette rings from The Bay Tree; serviettes and wooden trivet from Made Where. Right: China from Christofle.

BACON AND CHIVE SOUFFLES WITH CHEESE SAUCE

1 tablespoon packaged breadcrumbs
4 bacon rashers, chopped
20g butter
2 teaspoons plain flour
¼ teaspoon seasoned pepper
⅓ cup milk
2 tablespoons chopped fresh chives
2 teaspoons seeded mustard
2 eggs, separated

CHEESE SAUCE
⅓ cup sour cream
¼ cup grated parmesan cheese
2 tablespoons water

Grease 2 souffle dishes (1 cup capacity), sprinkle with breadcrumbs, shake away excess breadcrumbs. Place dishes on oven tray.

Add bacon to hot pan, cook, stirring, until bacon is crisp; drain on absorbent paper. Heat butter in clean pan, add flour and pepper, cook, stirring, until mixture is bubbly. Remove from heat, gradually stir in milk; stir over heat until mixture boils and thickens. Transfer mixture to large bowl, stir in bacon, chives, mustard and egg yolks.

Beat egg whites in small bowl until soft peaks form, fold gently into bacon mixture in 2 batches. Pour mixture into prepared dishes. Bake, uncovered, in moderately hot oven about 18 minutes or until well risen and firm to touch. Serve immediately with cheese sauce.

Cheese Sauce: Combine cream, cheese and water in pan, stir over heat, without boiling, until cheese is melted and sauce is heated through.

- Recipe must be made just before serving.
- Freeze: Not suitable.
- Microwave: Cheese sauce suitable.

SMOKED TROUT PARCELS WITH CREAMY DILL SAUCE

6 leaves English spinach
1 small smoked trout
2 teaspoons drained capers, chopped
2 sheets fillo pastry
50g butter, melted

CREAMY DILL SAUCE
2 tablespoons choppped fresh dill
⅓ cup sour cream
1 teaspoon horseradish cream
1 teaspoon seeded mustard

Add spinach to pan of boiling water, drain immediately, rinse under cold water, drain well; pat dry with absorbent paper.

Remove skin and bones from trout. Divide trout into 2 portions, top each portion with capers, wrap each portion in spinach leaves.

Brush 1 pastry sheet with butter, cut lengthways into 3 equal pieces. Layer pieces at an angle on top of each other. Place trout in spinach in centre of pastry, gather edges together to form a parcel, brush with butter. Repeat with remaining pastry, butter and trout in spinach. Place parcels on greased oven tray. Bake, uncovered, in moderate oven about 15 minutes or until browned. Serve with creamy dill sauce.

Creamy Dill Sauce: Combine all ingredients in bowl; mix well.

- Recipe can be prepared 3 hours ahead.
- Storage: Covered, in refrigerator.
- Freeze: Not suitable.
- Microwave: Spinach suitable.

LEFT: Bacon and Chive Souffles with Cheese Sauce.
RIGHT: Smoked Trout Parcels with Creamy Dill Sauce.

PRAWN AND CRAB SALAD WITH LIME DRESSING

80g green beans
10 cooked prawns
200g can crab meat, drained
1 orange, segmented

LIME DRESSING
1 clove garlic, crushed
¼ teaspoon shrimp paste
2 teaspoons fish sauce
2 tablespoons lime juice
**1 tablespoon chopped fresh
    coriander**
1 tablespoon chopped fresh mint
2 tablespoons oil

Boil, steam or microwave beans until just tender, rinse under cold water; drain, pat dry with absorbent paper. Shell and devein prawns, leaving tails intact.

Place beans, prawns, crab and orange segments on serving plates, pour over lime dressing.

Lime Dressing: Blend or process all ingredients until well combined.

■ Recipe best made just before serving.
■ Freeze: Not suitable.
■ Microwave: Beans suitable.

SEAFOOD PLATTER WITH HORSERADISH CREAM

The main ingredients can be bought from a delicatessen and assembled quickly to serve with drinks or as an entree.
3 slices brown bread, toasted
2 rollmop herrings
6 bottled mussels, drained
6 slices smoked salmon
110g can smoked eel, drained
6 fresh oysters in half shells

HORSERADISH CREAM
½ cup sour cream
1 tablespoon horseradish cream

Remove crusts from toast, cut toast into quarters. Place toast and seafood on platter. Serve with horseradish cream.

Horseradish Cream: Combine ingredients in bowl; mix well.

■ Recipe best prepared close to serving. Horseradish cream can be made a day ahead.
■ Storage: Covered, in refrigerator.
■ Freeze: Not suitable.

SAVOURY PLATTER WITH MARINATED MUSHROOMS

Buy the main ingredients from a delicatessen for this quick-to-assemble platter to serve with drinks or as an entree. The mushrooms need to be marinated for several hours or overnight.
3 pickled onions, drained, halved
3 artichoke hearts, drained, halved
¼ cup drained sun-dried tomatoes
¼ cup black olives
3 dill pickles
70g sliced salami
70g pate

PESTO
1 cup firmly packed fresh basil
¼ cup pine nuts, toasted
2 cloves garlic, crushed
½ cup olive oil
**2 tablespoons grated parmesan
    cheese**

MARINATED MUSHROOMS
2 tablespoons olive oil
2 cloves garlic, crushed
200g baby mushrooms
⅓ cup lemon juice
2 tablespoons olive oil, extra
**1 tablespoon chopped fresh
    marjoram**

Place onions, artichokes, tomatoes, olives, pickles, salami and pate on platter. Serve with pesto and mushrooms.

Pesto: Blend or process all ingredients until smooth.

Marinated Mushrooms: Heat oil and garlic in pan, add mushrooms, cook, stirring, until mushrooms are just tender. Pour undrained mushrooms into bowl, stir in juice, extra oil and marjoram, cover, refrigerate 3 hours or overnight.

■ Platter best assembled just before serving. Pesto can be made 2 days ahead. Marinated mushrooms can be made 7 days ahead.
■ Storage: Covered, in refrigerator.
■ Freeze: Not suitable.
■ Microwave: Mushrooms suitable.

LEFT: Prawn and Crab Salad with Lime Dressing.
RIGHT: From left: Seafood Platter with Horseradish Cream, Savoury Platter with Marinated Mushrooms.

ROAST POTATOES
WITH THREE TOPPINGS

Each topping is enough for 2 potatoes; make the topping of your choice.

2 medium (about 300g) potatoes

MUSHROOM HAM TOPPING
20g butter
½ onion, chopped
60g mushrooms, sliced
60g ham, chopped
1 tablespoon plain flour
½ cup milk
1 tablespoon chopped fresh parsley

AVOCADO TUNA TOPPING
½ medium avocado
¼ cup sour cream
1 tablespoon lemon juice

1 green shallot, chopped
100g can tuna, drained, flaked
2 teaspoons chopped fresh chives

ANCHOVY CHEESE TOPPING
2 tomatoes, peeled, seeded, chopped
½ onion, chopped
60g firm blue cheese, crumbled
2 anchovy fillets, drained, finely chopped
2 teaspoons chopped fresh basil

Place potatoes on oven tray, bake, uncovered, in moderate oven about 1 hour or until potatoes are tender. Cut a cross on top of potatoes, add desired topping.
Mushroom Ham Topping: Heat butter in pan, add onion, mushrooms and ham, cook, stirring, until onion is soft. Stir in flour, stir over heat until combined.

Remove from heat, gradually stir in milk. Stir over heat until mixture boils and thickens. Stir in parsley.
Avocado Tuna Topping: Blend or process avocado, cream and juice until smooth. Transfer mixture to bowl, stir in shallot, tuna and chives; mix well.
Anchovy Cheese Topping: Combine all ingredients in bowl; mix well.
■ Toppings best made just before serving.
■ Freeze: Not suitable.
■ Microwave: Potatoes suitable.

POTATO HASH WITH SMOKED SALMON AND POACHED EGG

2 large (about 400g) potatoes, grated
1 egg, lightly beaten
2 tablespoons oil
20g butter
½ medium leek, sliced
2 eggs, extra
100g smoked salmon

Squeeze excess moisture from potatoes, combine with egg in bowl; mix well. Heat oil in pan, add half the potato mixture; shape into a 10cm round. Cook slowly until browned underneath, turn, brown other side; drain on absorbent paper. Repeat with remaining potato mixture.

Heat butter in pan, add leek, cook, stirring, until soft. Place each potato hash on a serving plate, top with leek.

Poach extra eggs until cooked as desired, place over leek. Serve with smoked salmon.

■ Recipe best made just before serving.
■ Freeze: Not suitable.
■ Microwave: Leek and eggs suitable.

LEFT: Roast Potatoes with Three Toppings: From left: Mushroom Ham Topping, Anchovy Cheese Topping, Avocado Tuna Topping. BELOW: Potato Hash with Smoked Salmon and Poached Egg.

Below: Plate from Butler and Co.; tray from Home & Garden.

CORN CROQUETTES

30g butter
1 green shallot, chopped
¼ cup plain flour
⅔ cup milk
pinch nutmeg
1 slice ham, chopped
½ cup canned drained corn kernels
plain flour, extra
1 egg, lightly beaten
⅔ cup stale breadcrumbs
oil for deep-frying

Heat butter in pan, add shallot and flour, cook, stirring, until mixture is dry and grainy. Remove from heat, gradually stir in milk and nutmeg, stir over heat until mixture boils and thickens, stir in ham and corn. (Mixture should be quite thick.) Transfer mixture to bowl; cool, cover, refrigerate until cold.

Divide mixture into 6 portions, shape into croquettes using floured hands. Toss croquettes in extra flour, shake away excess flour, dip into egg, toss in breadcrumbs, refrigerate 15 minutes. Deep-fry croquettes in hot oil until browned.

Makes 6.

- ■ Croquettes can be prepared a day ahead.
- ■ Storage: Covered, in refrigerator.
- ■ Freeze: Uncooked croquettes suitable.
- ■ Microwave: Not suitable.

CORN BREAD, TOFU AND SALAD SANDWICH

½ cup drained corn kernels
100g tofu, crumbled
½ small red Spanish onion, finely chopped
2 tablespoons drained sliced sun-dried tomatoes
1 small dill pickle, finely chopped
1 small carrot, finely chopped
¼ small red pepper, finely chopped
1 tablespoon chopped fresh dill
1 tablespoon chopped fresh parsley
1 tablespoon chopped fresh chives
2 tablespoons mayonnaise
½ teaspoon seeded mustard
4 slices corn bread
2 lettuce leaves
1 small tomato, sliced

Combine corn, tofu, onion, sun-dried tomatoes, pickle, carrot, pepper, herbs, mayonnaise and mustard in bowl; mix well. Top 2 slices of bread with lettuce and tomato, top with corn mixture then remaining bread slices.

- ■ Recipe best made just before serving.
- ■ Freeze: Not suitable.

RIGHT: From top: Corn Bread, Tofu and Salad Sandwich, Corn Croquettes, Beef on Parmesan Toast with Shallot Cream.

BEEF ON PARMESAN TOAST WITH SHALLOT CREAM

2 slices bread, toasted
2 tablespoons grated parmesan
   cheese
250g sirloin steak

SHALLOT CREAM
20g butter
2 green shallots, chopped
¼ cup sour cream
½ teaspoon Worcestershire sauce
few drops tabasco sauce

Sprinkle toast with cheese, grill until melted. Grill steak until done as desired; cool 10 minutes, slice thinly. Divide steak between toasts, top with shallot cream.
Shallot Cream: Heat butter in pan, add shallots, cook, stirring, until soft. Stir in cream and sauces, stir over heat until heated through.

- Recipe best made just before serving.
- Freeze: Not suitable.
- Microwave: Shallot cream suitable.

SOUFFLE OMELETTE WITH MUSHROOM SAUCE

4 eggs, separated
1 tablespoon water
2 teaspoons chopped fresh tarragon
20g butter

MUSHROOM SAUCE
60g butter
1 small onion, chopped
1 clove garlic, crushed
125g baby mushrooms, sliced
3 teaspoons plain flour
¼ cup dry white wine
½ cup chicken stock
¼ cup milk
2 teaspoons French mustard
2 teaspoons chopped fresh tarragon

Whisk egg yolks, water and tarragon in large bowl until well combined. Beat egg whites in small bowl with electric mixer until soft peaks form. Fold egg whites gently into egg yolk mixture in 2 batches.

Heat half the butter in omelette pan. Pour half the egg mixture into pan, cook omelette until lightly browned underneath.

Place pan under hot grill until top of omelette is just set. Slide omelette onto plate, fold omelette in half, spoon over half the mushroom sauce. Repeat with remaining butter, egg mixture and sauce.
Mushroom Sauce: Heat butter in pan, add onion, garlic and mushrooms, cook, stirring, until onion is soft. Add flour, cook, stirring, until combined. Remove from heat, gradually stir in combined remaining ingredients, stir over heat until mixture boils and thickens.

- Omelette best made just before serving. Mushroom sauce can be made a day ahead.
- Storage: Covered, in refrigerator.
- Freeze: Not suitable.
- Microwave: Sauce suitable.

BELOW: Souffle Omelette with Mushroom Sauce.

China and cutlery from Mikasa.

MINI POCKET PIZZAS WITH THREE TOPPINGS

Each topping is enough for 2 pita pocket breads; make the topping of your choice.

2 pita pocket breads

EGGPLANT CHEESE TOPPING
1 tablespoon oil
½ green pepper, sliced
1 clove garlic, crushed
½ onion, sliced
2 baby eggplants, sliced
2 tablespoons tomato paste
100g goats' cheese, crumbled

CABANOSSI OLIVE TOPPING
2 tablespoons tomato paste
1 tablespoon chopped fresh basil
1 stick cabanossi, sliced
8 black olives, halved
½ cup grated mozzarella cheese

BACON ARTICHOKE TOPPING
2 bacon rashers, chopped
2 tablespoons tomato paste
2 tablespoons drained chopped sun-dried tomatoes
4 artichoke hearts, drained, sliced
½ cup grated mozzarella cheese

Spread pocket breads with the topping of your choice, place pizzas on oven tray. Bake, uncovered, in moderately hot oven about 15 minutes or until heated through and lightly browned.

Eggplant Cheese Topping: Heat oil in pan, add pepper, garlic, onion and eggplants, cook, stirring, until vegetables are just tender. Spread bread with paste, top with eggplant mixture; top with cheese.

Cabanossi Olive Topping: Spread bread with tomato paste, top with basil, cabanossi, olives and cheese.

Bacon Artichoke Topping: Add bacon to hot pan, cook, stirring, until bacon is crisp; drain on absorbent paper. Spread bread with paste, top with bacon, tomatoes, artichokes and cheese.

- ■ Recipe best made just before serving.
- ■ Freeze: Suitable.
- ■ Microwave: Not suitable.

BELOW: Mini Pocket Pizzas with Three Toppings. From left: Bacon Artichoke Topping, Cabanossi Olive Topping, Eggplant Cheese Topping.
RIGHT: From left: Cheesy Tuna Rolls, Jaffles with Lamb and Pickle Filling.

Right: China from Mikasa.

CHEESY TUNA ROLLS

1 hard-boiled egg, finely chopped
95g can tuna, drained, flaked
2 teaspoons mayonnaise
**2 tablespoons drained canned
    diced capsicum**
1 teaspoon lemon juice
1 tablespoon chopped fresh chives
2 bread rolls
⅓ cup grated tasty cheese
20g butter, melted

Combine egg, tuna, mayonnaise, capsicum, juice and chives in bowl. Cut tops from rolls, spread with tuna mixture, sprinkle with cheese, cover with tops, press down gently. Place rolls on oven tray, brush with butter. Bake, uncovered, in moderately hot oven about 15 minutes or until cheese is melted.

- Filling can be prepared 6 hours ahead.
- Storage: Covered, in refrigerator.
- Freeze: Not suitable.
- Microwave: Not suitable.

JAFFLES WITH LAMB AND PICKLE FILLING

2 teaspoons oil
2 lamb cutlets
20g butter
4 slices bread
1 tablespoon seeded mustard
4 dill pickles, sliced
60g sliced tasty cheese

Heat oil in pan, add cutlets, cook until browned and tender; cool, slice.

Butter 1 side of each slice of bread. Place 2 slices of bread, butter side down, on board, spread each with mustard, top with lamb, pickles and cheese. Top both with remaining bread, butter side up. Cook in sandwich maker or jaffle iron until browned and heated through.

- Recipe best made just before serving.
- Freeze: Not suitable.
- Microwave: Not suitable.

POULTRY

We've used mainly chicken in this section, with quail, duck and spatchcocks adding

temptation to your choice. We've made them pretty and elegant, and simplified any tricky

procedures with step-by-step pictures. Some recipes are extra quick, such as lemon

mustard kebabs or sweet and sour chicken drumsticks. The same idea is reflected in the

accompaniments, some simple and others as smart as broccoli souffle tomatoes

and tangy marinated artichoke salad.

Herbed Chicken Salad
with Raspberry Vinaigrette

Thyme and Garlic Toasts

HERBED CHICKEN SALAD WITH RASPBERRY VINAIGRETTE

2 teaspoons olive oil
2 teaspoons tomato sauce
2 teaspoons lemon juice
1 tablespoon chopped fresh basil
1 tablespoon chopped fresh parsley
½ teaspoon seasoned pepper
2 chicken breast fillets
1 small radicchio lettuce
1 small butter lettuce

RASPBERRY VINAIGRETTE
½ cup frozen raspberries, thawed
½ teaspoon French mustard
2 tablespoons olive oil
3 teaspoons balsamic vinegar
½ teaspoon sugar

Combine oil, sauce, juice, herbs and pepper in bowl; mix well. Spread 1 side of each piece of chicken with half the herb mixture; reserve remaining herb mixture. Cover chicken, refrigerate 1 hour.

Grill chicken herb side up until browned, turn chicken, spread with reserved herb mixture, grill until tender; cool. Slice chicken, tear lettuce into pieces. Pour half the raspberry vinaigrette over lettuce in bowl, add chicken, drizzle with remaining vinaigrette. Serve with thyme and garlic toasts.

Raspberry Vinaigrette: Sieve berries, combine puree with remaining ingredients in jar; shake well.

■ Dressing can be made a day ahead.
■ Storage: Covered, in refrigerator.
■ Freeze: Not suitable.
■ Microwave: Not suitable.

THYME AND GARLIC TOASTS

20g soft butter
½ teaspoon dried thyme leaves
1 clove garlic, crushed
1 small French bread stick

Combine butter, thyme and garlic in bowl.

Cut bread into 6 thick diagonal slices. Spread bread with butter mixture, place in single layer on oven tray. Bake, uncovered, in moderate oven about 15 minutes or until crisp, turning once.

■ Recipe best made just before serving.
■ Freeze: Not suitable.
■ Microwave: Not suitable.

RIGHT: Herbed Chicken Salad with Raspberry Vinaigrette and Thyme and Garlic Toasts.

Bowl from Kenwick Galleries.

Seasoned Quail with Wild Rice

Buttered Vegetables

SEASONED QUAIL WITH WILD RICE

¼ cup wild rice
2 quail
1 tablespoon oil
20g butter
1 clove garlic, crushed
1 teaspoon grated fresh ginger
¼ cup dry white wine
¼ cup water
1 tablespoon honey
1 tablespoon light soy sauce
1 teaspoon cornflour
1 teaspoon water, extra

SEASONING
1 tablespoon oil
250g minced chicken
1 clove garlic, crushed
½ teaspoon grated fresh ginger
2 green shallots, chopped
2 tablespoons dry white wine
½ teaspoon chicken stock powder
¾ cup stale breadcrumbs
1 egg white, lightly beaten

Add rice to pan of boiling water, boil, uncovered, about 40 minutes or until rice is tender; drain, keep warm.

Using a sharp knife, cut along each side of backbone; remove and discard bone.

Place quail skin side down on board. Carefully cut through thigh joints and wing joints without cutting skin. Scrape meat away from rib cage.

Continue scraping meat from rib cage and breastbone; discard bones.

Place quail skin side down on bench, top with seasoning. Fold in sides of quail to overlap, secure with toothpicks. Tuck wings under body, tie legs together.

Heat oil and butter in flameproof pan, add quail, cook until browned all over. Bake, uncovered, in moderately hot oven about 20 minutes or until quail are tender.

Drain fat from pan, add garlic, ginger and wine, cook, stirring, 1 minute. Add water, honey, sauce and blended cornflour and extra water, stir over heat until mixture boils and thickens slightly; strain. Serve quail with wild rice and sauce, sprinkled with chopped basil, if desired. Serve with buttered vegetables.
Seasoning: Heat oil in pan, add mince, cook, stirring, until changed in colour. Add garlic, ginger, shallots, wine and stock powder, cook, stirring, until liquid is evaporated; cool. Stir in breadcrumbs and egg white.

- Recipe can be prepared a day ahead.
- Storage: Covered, in refrigerator.
- Freeze: Uncooked seasoned quail suitable.
- Microwave: Not suitable.

BUTTERED VEGETABLES

1 small leek
2 medium (about 240g) carrots
1 small red pepper
1 small yellow pepper
20g butter

Cut vegetables into thin strips. Heat butter in pan, add vegetables, cook, stirring, until vegetables are just tender.

- Recipe best made just before serving.
- Freeze: Not suitable.
- Microwave: Suitable.

LEFT: Seasoned Quail with Wild Rice and Buttered Vegetables.

China and glass from Wedgwood; silver plate from Mandina Imports.

Barbecued Quail

Marinated Artichoke Salad

BARBECUED QUAIL

4 quail
¼ cup lemon juice
2 tablespoons olive oil
1 small clove garlic, crushed
½ teaspoon dried oregano leaves

Cut quail into 4 portions. Combine quail with remaining ingredients in bowl, cover, refrigerate several hours or overnight.

Remove quail from marinade, discard marinade. Barbecue, grill or pan-fry quail until browned and tender. Serve quail with marinated artichoke salad.

■ Recipe can be prepared a day ahead.
■ Storage: Covered, in refrigerator.
■ Freeze: Not suitable.
■ Microwave: Not suitable.

MARINATED ARTICHOKE SALAD

275g jar artichoke hearts, drained, halved
6 spears fresh asparagus
1 small green cucumber
½ red pepper, sliced
2 cups watercress sprigs

DRESSING
2 tablespoons tarragon vinegar
2 tablespoons olive oil
½ teaspoon sugar
¼ teaspoon dried chilli flakes
¼ teaspoon seeded mustard

Combine artichoke hearts and dressing in bowl, cover, stand 1 hour.

Cut asparagus into 3cm lengths. Boil, steam, or microwave asparagus until tender; drain. Using a vegetable peeler, slice cucumber into ribbons. Combine artichoke mixture, asparagus, cucumber, pepper and watercress; mix well.

Dressing: Combine all ingredients in jar; shake well.

- Recipe can be prepared an hour ahead.
- Storage: Covered, at room temperature.
- Freeze: Not suitable.
- Microwave: Asparagus suitable.

Chicken and Vegetable Casserole

CHICKEN AND VEGETABLE CASSEROLE

1 tablespoon oil
4 chicken thigh cutlets
1 onion, chopped
1 clove garlic, crushed
2 small carrots, sliced
1 stick celery, sliced
400g can tomatoes
1 teaspoon chicken stock powder
1 teaspoon Worcestershire sauce
½ teaspoon sugar
1 zucchini, sliced
1 tablespoon chopped fresh basil
2 tablespoons grated parmesan cheese

Heat oil in pan, add chicken, cook until browned all over; remove from pan.

Add onion, garlic, carrots and celery to pan, cook, stirring, until onion is soft. Stir in undrained crushed tomatoes, stock powder, sauce and sugar, then chicken and zucchini. Simmer, covered, until chicken is tender. Stir in basil and cheese. Serve casserole with crusty bread.

- Recipe can be made a day ahead.
- Storage: Covered, in refrigerator.
- Freeze: Suitable.
- Microwave: Not suitable.

LEFT: From top: Marinated Artichoke Salad, Barbecued Quail.
BELOW: Chicken and Vegetable Casserole

Left: China and cutlery from The Bay Tree; serviette from Country Road Homewares; salt and pepper set from Bibelot; tiles from Pazotti.

Chilli Coconut Chicken Curry

Brown Rice

Baked Kumara

CHILLI COCONUT CHICKEN CURRY

30g butter
2 (about 300g) chicken thigh fillets, sliced
1 large (about 200g) onion, sliced
1 clove garlic, crushed
1 tablespoon chopped fresh lemon grass
½ teaspoon red chilli flakes
2 teaspoons chopped fresh coriander
2 teaspoons lime juice
½ teaspoon cumin seeds
½ teaspoon turmeric
½ teaspoon fish sauce
1 teaspoon sugar
2 teaspoons plain flour
1 teaspoon chicken stock powder
¾ cup coconut milk

Heat butter in pan, add chicken, cook, stirring, until browned and tender; drain on absorbent paper.

Reheat pan, add onion, garlic, lemon grass, chilli, coriander, juice, seeds, turmeric and sauce, cook, stirring, until onion is soft. Stir in chicken, sugar and flour, then stock powder and milk, stir over heat until mixture boils and thickens. Serve with brown rice and baked kumara.

■ Recipe can be made 3 hours ahead.
■ Storage: Covered, in refrigerator.
■ Freeze: Suitable.
■ Microwave: Not suitable.

BROWN RICE

⅔ cup brown rice

Add rice to pan of boiling water, boil, uncovered, about 30 minutes or until tender; drain.

■ Rice can be cooked a day ahead.
■ Storage: Covered, in refrigerator.
■ Freeze: Suitable.
■ Microwave: Suitable.

BAKED KUMARA

300g kumara
1 tablespoon olive oil
½ teaspoon cumin seeds

Cut kumara into 5mm slices. Cut slices into 3cm strips.

Combine kumara, oil and seeds in bowl. Transfer mixture to baking dish. Bake, uncovered, in hot oven 10 minutes, turn kumara, reduce heat to moderately hot, bake further 20 minutes or until kumara is tender.

■ Recipe best made just before serving.
■ Freeze: Not suitable.
■ Microwave: Not suitable.

LEFT: Chilli Coconut Chicken Curry with Baked Kumara and Brown Rice.

Chicken with Apples, Currants and Cream

Pasta with Spinach and Almonds

CHICKEN WITH APPLES, CURRANTS AND CREAM

2 chicken breast fillets
1 tablespoon oil
2 small (about 220g) apples, peeled, sliced
2 tablespoons currants
2 teaspoons chopped fresh tarragon
1½ tablespoons Calvados
⅔ cup cream

Flatten chicken with meat mallet between sheets of greaseproof paper. Heat oil in pan, add chicken, cook until browned and tender; remove from pan.

Reheat pan, add apples, cook, stirring occasionally, until browned and just tender. Add currants, tarragon, brandy and cream, simmer, uncovered, until sauce is slightly thickened. Serve sauce and apples over chicken. Serve with pasta with spinach and almonds.

- Recipe best made just before serving.
- Freeze: Not suitable.
- Microwave: Suitable.

PASTA WITH SPINACH AND ALMONDS

50g tomato fettucine pasta
20g butter
12 leaves English spinach
1½ tablespoons flaked almonds, toasted

Add pasta to pan of boiling water, simmer, uncovered, until just tender; drain.

Heat butter in pan, add pasta, spinach and almonds, toss gently over heat until spinach is wilted and pasta hot.

- Recipe best made just before serving.
- Freeze: Not suitable.
- Microwave: Suitable.

ABOVE: Chicken with Apples, Currants and Cream and Pasta with Spinach and Almonds.

Plate from Mikasa.

Chicken with Tangy Cheese Seasoning

Broccoli Souffle Tomatoes

CHICKEN WITH TANGY CHEESE SEASONING

60g goats' cheese, chopped
2 green shallots, chopped
1 tablespoon chopped fresh basil
2 chicken breast fillets
1 tablespoon oil

MUSHROOM SAUCE
30g butter
100g baby mushrooms, sliced
2 tablespoons dry white wine
½ cup cream
½ teaspoon seeded mustard
2 teaspoons chopped fresh chives

Combine cheese, shallots and basil in bowl; mix well. Cut pocket in side of chicken fillets; fill with cheese mixture; secure with toothpicks. Heat oil in pan, add chicken, cook until lightly browned and tender. Serve with mushroom sauce and broccoli souffle tomatoes.

Mushroom Sauce: Heat butter in pan, add mushrooms, cook, stirring, until lightly browned. Stir in wine, cream and mustard, simmer, uncovered, until slightly thickened. Stir in chives.

- Chicken can be prepared a day ahead. Mushroom sauce best made just before serving.
- Storage: Covered, in refrigerator.
- Freeze: Uncooked seasoned chicken suitable.
- Microwave: Sauce suitable.

BROCCOLI SOUFFLE TOMATOES

1 large (about 250g) tomato
50g broccoli
20g butter
1 green shallot, chopped
1 tablespoon plain flour
½ cup milk
¼ teaspoon seeded mustard
1 egg yolk
2 egg whites

Cut tomato in half, scoop out seeds, discard seeds. Place tomato halves on oven tray. Boil, steam or microwave broccoli until soft; drain, chop finely.

Heat butter in pan, add shallot, cook, stirring, until soft. Stir in flour, cook until bubbling. Remove from heat, gradually stir in milk and mustard; stir over heat until sauce boils and thickens; cool slightly. Stir in broccoli and egg yolk.

Beat egg whites in small bowl until soft peaks form, fold into broccoli mixture in 2 batches. Spoon broccoli mixture into tomato halves. Bake, uncovered, in hot oven about 8 minutes or until puffed and lightly browned.

- Recipe must be made just before serving.
- Freeze: Not suitable.
- Microwave: Broccoli suitable.

ABOVE: Chicken with Tangy Cheese Seasoning and Broccoli Souffle Tomatoes.

Lemon Mustard Kebabs with Peppers

Corn Bread Muffins

LEMON MUSTARD KEBABS WITH PEPPERS

2 (about 300g) chicken thigh fillets
1 red pepper
1 green pepper

MARINADE
2 teaspoons grated lemon rind
2 tablespoons lemon juice
1 tablespoon seeded mustard
2 teaspoons chopped fresh rosemary
1 tablespoon olive oil
2 cloves garlic, crushed
1 tablespoon honey

Cut chicken into long thin strips, pound lightly to flatten. Combine chicken and marinade in bowl, cover, refrigerate several hours or overnight.

Quarter peppers, remove seeds and membrane. Grill peppers skin side up until skin blisters and blackens. Peel away and discard skin.

Drain chicken from marinade, reserve marinade; thread chicken onto 6 skewers. Grill kebabs until tender, brushing with some of the reserved marinade during cooking. Brush peppers with remaining marinade, grill or microwave to reheat. Serve peppers with kebabs. Serve with corn bread muffins.

Marinade: Combine all ingredients in bowl; mix well.

■ Recipe can be prepared a day ahead.
■ Storage: Covered, in refrigerator.
■ Freeze: Marinated chicken suitable.
■ Microwave: Kebabs suitable.

CORN BREAD MUFFINS

½ cup cornmeal
⅓ cup self-raising flour
1 tablespoon sugar
½ teaspoon ground cumin
pinch chilli powder
¼ teaspoon seasoned pepper
1 tablespoon chopped fresh parsley
1 egg, lightly beaten
20g butter, melted
⅓ cup milk
2 teaspoons cornmeal, extra

Lightly grease 4 holes (⅓ cup capacity) of muffin pan.

Sift dry ingredients into bowl, stir in pepper, parsley, egg, butter and milk; mix until just combined. Spoon mixture into prepared pan, sprinkle with extra cornmeal. Bake in moderate oven about 30 minutes or until lightly browned and cooked through.

■ Recipe can be made 2 days ahead.
■ Storage: Airtight container.
■ Freeze: Suitable.
■ Microwave: Not suitable.

RIGHT: Lemon Mustard Kebabs with Peppers and Corn Bread Muffins.

Plate and salt and pepper set from Bibelot; tiles from Pazotti.

Chicken Ballotines

Tomato Lentils

CHICKEN BALLOTINES

2 chicken marylands
2 teaspoons oil

SEASONING
1 chicken breast fillet, chopped
1 clove garlic, crushed
1 tablespoon chopped fresh chives
1 tablespoon chopped fresh tarragon
1 egg white
1 tablespoon cream

Starting from the thigh end of each maryland, run sharp knife along thigh and along leg, exposing bones. Remove a little flesh from end of thigh bone. Holding thigh bone, scrape flesh away from bone.

Cut through joint only, not through flesh. Remove thigh bone.

Holding thin end of leg, scrape flesh back to joint, remove bone. Flesh should be intact.

Place each chicken piece skin side down on bench, place half seasoning on each piece, wrap chicken around seasoning to enclose, sew together with needle and thread or secure with toothpicks.

Place ballotines on wire rack in baking dish, brush with oil. Bake, uncovered, in moderate oven about 45 minutes or until tender. Serve with tomato lentils.

Seasoning: Process all ingredients until smooth, cover, refrigerate 30 minutes.

■ Chicken can be prepared a day ahead.
■ Storage: Covered, in refrigerator.
■ Freeze: Uncooked seasoned chicken suitable.
■ Microwave: Not suitable.

TOMATO LENTILS

1 tablespoon oil
1 small onion, chopped
1 clove garlic, crushed
1 small carrot, chopped
1 cup (200g) red lentils
2 cups chicken stock
½ teaspoon ground cumin
1 tomato, peeled, seeded, chopped
2 teaspoons chopped fresh tarragon

Heat oil in pan, add onion, garlic and carrot, cook, stirring, until onion is soft. Add lentils, stock and cumin, simmer, covered, until lentils are tender. Stir in tomato and tarragon; stir until hot.

■ Recipe can be prepared a day ahead.
■ Storage: Covered, in refrigerator.
■ Freeze: Suitable.
■ Microwave: Suitable.

BELOW: Chicken Ballotines with Tomato Lentils.

Roast Seasoned Spatchcocks

Zucchini and Eggplant Fritters

ROAST SEASONED SPATCHCOCKS

1 teaspoon seeded mustard
50g soft butter
1 tablespoon chopped fresh basil
2 tablespoons pine nuts, chopped
1 tablespoon drained chopped sun-dried tomatoes
1 tablespoon chopped raisins
1 tablespoon grated parmesan cheese
1 cup (70g) stale breadcrumbs
2 x 400g spatchcocks
20g butter, melted, extra
¼ cup dry white wine
½ teaspoon chicken stock powder
¼ teaspoon sugar
2 tablespoons cream

Combine mustard, butter, basil, nuts, tomatoes, raisins, cheese and breadcrumbs in bowl; mix well. Loosen skin of spatchcocks by sliding finger between skin and flesh at neck joint and over breastbone. Gently push seasoning evenly under skin. Tuck wings under bodies, tie legs together. Place spatchcocks on wire rack in baking dish, brush with half the extra butter, cover breasts with foil. Bake in moderate oven 30 minutes, remove foil, brush with remaining extra butter, bake about 15 minutes or until tender.

Remove spatchcocks from dish, reheat juices. Add wine, stock powder and sugar, bring to boil. Stir in cream, cook, stirring, until slightly thickened; strain. Serve sauce with spatchcocks. Serve with zucchini and eggplant fritters.

- Recipe can be prepared a day ahead.
- Storage: Covered, in refrigerator.
- Freeze: Uncooked seasoned spatchcocks suitable.
- Microwave: Not suitable.

ZUCCHINI AND EGGPLANT FRITTERS

2 small (about 100g) zucchini
2 baby eggplants
1 egg
¼ cup cornflour
¼ cup plain flour
¼ cup water
plain flour, extra
oil for deep-frying

Cut zucchini and eggplants in half lengthways.

Beat egg in small bowl until thick and creamy, fold in sifted flours and water in 2 batches. Toss vegetables in extra flour, shake away excess flour, dip vegetables in batter. Deep-fry vegetables in hot oil until browned, drain on absorbent paper.

- Recipe best made just before serving.
- Freeze: Not suitable.
- Microwave: Not suitable.

ABOVE: Roast Seasoned Spatchcocks with Zucchini and Eggplant Fritters.

Sweet and Sour Chicken Drumsticks

Fried Rice

SWEET AND SOUR CHICKEN DRUMSTICKS

4 chicken drumsticks
1 tablespoon light soy sauce
2 teaspoons dry sherry
2 teaspoons oil

SWEET AND SOUR SAUCE
½ cup pineapple juice
1 tablespoon tomato sauce
1 teaspoon light soy sauce
1 tablespoon white vinegar
1 tablespoon sugar
1 clove garlic, crushed
2 teaspoons cornflour
1 tablespoon water
½ small green pepper, chopped
½ small red pepper, chopped
1 green shallot, chopped

Combine chicken with remaining ingredients in bowl, cover, stand 1 hour.

Drain chicken, reserve marinade. Place chicken on wire rack in baking dish. Bake, uncovered, in moderate oven about 30 minutes or until browned and tender. Brush with reserved marinade during cooking. Serve with sweet and sour sauce and fried rice.

Sweet and Sour Sauce: Combine juice, sauces, vinegar, sugar and garlic in pan, simmer, uncovered, 5 minutes. Stir in blended cornflour and water, peppers and shallot, stir over heat until sauce boils and thickens slightly.

- Recipe can be made a day ahead.
- Storage: Covered, in refrigerator.
- Freeze: Suitable.
- Microwave: Sauce suitable.

FRIED RICE

¾ cup long-grain rice
30g butter
1 small onion, finely chopped
8 baby mushrooms, halved
½ cup frozen peas
⅓ cup roasted cashews
2 teaspoons light soy sauce

Add rice to pan of boiling water, boil, uncovered, until just tender, rinse under cold water; drain.

Heat butter in pan, add onion, cook, stirring, until soft, add mushrooms, peas and nuts, cook, stirring, 2 minutes, stir in rice and sauce, stir until heated through.

- Recipe can be made a day ahead.
- Storage: Covered, in refrigerator.
- Freeze: Suitable.
- Microwave: Suitable.

Quail in Honey Sherry Marinade

Stir-Fried Vegetables

Deep-Fried Vermicelli

QUAIL IN HONEY SHERRY MARINADE

4 quail

HONEY SHERRY MARINADE
2 tablespoons honey
¼ cup light soy sauce
2 cloves garlic, crushed
1 teaspoon grated fresh ginger
2 tablespoons dry sherry
½ teaspoon grated lime rind

Cut quail in half; combine in bowl with marinade, cover, refrigerate several hours or overnight.

Drain quail, reserve marinade. Place quail skin side up on wire rack in baking dish. Bake in moderately hot oven about 20 minutes or until tender. Boil reserved marinade in pan; strain. Serve quail with deep-fried vermicelli and stir-fried vegetables; pour over marinade.
Honey Sherry Marinade: Combine all ingredients in bowl; mix well.

- Quail can be prepared a day ahead.
- Storage: Covered, in refrigerator.
- Freeze: Marinated quail suitable.
- Microwave: Not suitable.

STIR-FRIED VEGETABLES

½ bunch (6 spears) fresh asparagus
½ small red pepper
1 zucchini
30g butter

Cut vegetables into very fine strips the same length. Heat butter in pan, add vegetables, cook, stirring, until tender.

- Vegetables are best made just before serving.
- Freeze: Not suitable.
- Microwave: Suitable.

DEEP-FRIED VERMICELLI

oil for deep-frying
50g rice vermicelli

Heat oil in pan, deep-fry vermicelli until puffed and white in colour; drain on absorbent paper.

- Vermicelli can be made a day ahead.
- Storage: Airtight container.
- Freeze: Not suitable.
- Microwave: Not suitable.

FAR LEFT: Sweet and Sour Chicken Drumsticks with Fried Rice.
LEFT: Quail in Honey Sherry Marinade with Stir-Fried Vegetables and Deep-Fried Vermicelli.

Far left: China and fork from The Bay Tree.
Left: Plate from The Bay Tree; place mats, serviette and cutlery from County Road Homewares; serviette ring and Alessi basket from Bibelot; tiles from Pazotti.

CHICKEN IN COCONUT LIME MARINADE

4 chicken thigh cutlets
1 cup chicken stock

COCONUT LIME MARINADE
1 tablespoon lime juice
150g can coconut milk
1 tablespoon chopped fresh coriander
1 clove garlic, crushed
1 teaspoon grated fresh ginger

Combine chicken and marinade in bowl; cover, refrigerate 1 hour or overnight.

Remove chicken from marinade, reserve marinade. Place chicken on wire rack in baking dish. Bake, uncovered, in moderate oven about 20 minutes or until browned and tender.

Combine reserved marinade and stock in pan, simmer, uncovered, until reduced by half. Serve sauce over chicken. Serve with vegetables in noodle baskets.

Coconut Lime Marinade: Combine all ingredients in bowl; mix well.

- Recipe can be prepared a day ahead.
- Storage: Covered, in refrigerator.
- Freeze: Not suitable.
- Microwave: Not suitable.

VEGETABLES IN NOODLE BASKETS

125g fresh egg noodles
oil for deep-frying

VEGETABLES
2 teaspoons oil
1 clove garlic, crushed
½ small red pepper, thinly sliced
½ small yellow pepper, thinly sliced
50g snow peas, thinly sliced
150g oyster mushrooms, thinly sliced
2 tablespoons light soy sauce
50g bean sprouts

Arrange half the noodles in a thin layer over the inside of lightly oiled double strainer. Press top strainer onto noodles. Lower strainer into hot oil, holding handles firmly together, deep-fry until noodles are well browned; drain.

Carefully remove noodle basket from strainer. Repeat with remaining noodles. Spoon vegetables into baskets.

Vegetables: Heat oil in pan or wok, add garlic, peppers, snow peas, mushrooms, sauce and sprouts, stir-fry vegetables until heated through and just tender.

- Baskets can be made a day ahead.
- Storage: Airtight container.
- Freeze: Not suitable.
- Microwave: Vegetables suitable.

LEFT: Chicken in Coconut Lime Marinade and Vegetables in Noodle Baskets.

Marinated Duck with Mango Salsa

Green Salad with Balsamic Dressing

MARINATED DUCK WITH MANGO SALSA

2 duck breast fillets
1 tablespoon oil

MARINADE
1 tablespoon chopped fresh
**   lemon grass**
2 tablespoons lemon juice
1 clove garlic, crushed
1 teaspoon seasoned pepper
1 tablespoon oil

MANGO SALSA
½ small red Spanish onion, chopped
1 small mango, chopped
1 teaspoon chopped fresh coriander
1 tablespoon lemon juice
1 teaspoon grated fresh ginger
½ teaspoon chilli sauce
¾ teaspoon sugar

Combine duck breasts and marinade in bowl; cover, refrigerate several hours or overnight.

Prick duck skin all over with skewer. Heat oil in pan, add duck and marinade, cook until duck is browned and tender. Serve duck sliced with mango salsa.

Marinade: Combine all ingredients in bowl; mix well.

Mango Salsa: Combine all ingredients in bowl, cover, refrigerate 1 hour.

■ Recipe can be prepared a day ahead.
■ Storage: Covered, in refrigerator.
■ Freeze: Marinated duck suitable.
■ Microwave: Not suitable.

GREEN SALAD WITH BALSAMIC DRESSING

1 bacon rasher
2 slices bread
30g butter, melted
2 radicchio lettuce leaves
8 rocket lettuce leaves
½ cup watercress sprigs

BALSAMIC DRESSING
2 tablespoons lemon juice
1 tablespoon balsamic vinegar
1 teaspoon honey

Cut bacon into thin strips, cook in hot pan until crisp; drain, cool. Remove crusts from bread, cut bread into 1cm cubes, toss in butter, place on oven tray. Bake, uncovered, in moderately hot oven about 8 minutes or until lightly browned. Drain croutons on absorbent paper, cool.

Combine torn lettuce leaves, watercress, bacon and croutons in bowl, drizzle with balsamic dressing.

Balsamic Dressing: Combine all ingredients in jar; shake well.

■ Recipe best made just before serving.
■ Freeze: Not suitable.
■ Microwave: Bacon suitable.

ABOVE: Marinated Duck with Mango Salsa and Green Salad with Balsamic Dressing.

China and cutlery from The Bay Tree; place mats from Country Road Homewares.

*Crusty Parmesan Chicken on
Tomato and Eggplant*

Green Pea Risotto

CRUSTY PARMESAN CHICKEN ON TOMATO AND EGGPLANT

2 teaspoons olive oil
½ teaspoon seeded mustard
1 clove garlic, crushed
2 teaspoons chopped fresh basil
2 teaspoons chopped fresh parsley
2 chicken breast fillets
1 tablespoon grated parmesan
  cheese
1 tablespoon stale breadcrumbs
½ medium (about 150g) eggplant
1 medium (about 130g) tomato
coarse cooking salt
1 tablespoon olive oil, extra
1 teaspoon lemon juice

Combine oil, mustard, garlic and herbs in bowl, add chicken, mix well, cover, refrigerate 1 hour.

Combine cheese and breadcrumbs in bowl, press mixture firmly onto chicken.

Cut eggplant and tomato into 1½cm slices (you will need 4 slices of each).

Sprinkle eggplant with salt, stand 30 minutes. Rinse under cold water, drain.

Place chicken and eggplant separately on wire rack in baking dish, brush both with extra oil. Bake, uncovered, in moderately hot oven 25 minutes. Turn eggplant, top with tomato slices, brush with a little more extra oil, bake further 10 minutes or until chicken is tender and vegetables hot. Serve chicken on layered eggplant and tomato; sprinkle with juice. Serve with green pea risotto.

- Chicken can be prepared a day ahead. Vegetables best cooked just before serving.
- Storage: Covered, in refrigerator.
- Freeze: Uncooked crumbed chicken suitable.
- Microwave: Not suitable.

BELOW: Crusty Parmesan Chicken on Tomato and Eggplant with Green Pea Risotto.

Plate and paper from Bibelot; tiles from Pazotti.

GREEN PEA RISOTTO

1 tablespoon olive oil
½ green pepper, chopped
½ small leek, chopped
½ cup frozen peas, thawed
15g butter
⅓ cup rice
2 tablespoons dry white wine
2¼ cups chicken stock

Heat oil in pan, add pepper and leek, cook, stirring, until pepper is soft; stir in peas. Transfer mixture to bowl.

Heat butter in same pan, add rice, stir until coated in butter, add wine, cook, stirring, until almost all the liquid is absorbed. Gradually add stock, about ¼ cup at a time, stirring constantly and allowing almost all the water to be absorbed before next addition. When rice is tender, stir in pea mixture, stir until heated through.

- Recipe best made just before serving.
- Freeze: Not suitable
- Microwave: Not suitable.

Chicken with Olives and Prunes

Pan-Fried Potatoes

Rocket and Radicchio Salad

CHICKEN WITH OLIVES AND PRUNES

2 chicken thigh cutlets
2 chicken drumsticks
¼ cup plain flour
1 teaspoon dried oregano leaves
2 tablespoons oil
1 tablespoon drained capers
⅓ cup pitted prunes
12 pimiento-stuffed green olives
⅓ cup dry white wine
2 tablespoons red wine vinegar
1 tablespoon brown sugar
1 tablespoon tomato paste
1 teaspoon dried oregano
    leaves, extra
1 tablespoon chopped fresh parsley
1 tablespoon sour cream

Toss chicken in combined flour and oregano, shake away excess flour. Heat oil in pan, add chicken, cook until browned all over; drain on absorbent paper.

Transfer chicken to heatproof dish (4 cup capacity). Add capers, prunes, olives, wine, vinegar, sugar, paste, extra oregano and parsley. Bake, covered, in moderate oven about 30 minutes or until chicken is tender. Stir in sour cream. Serve chicken with pan-fried potatoes and rocket and radicchio salad.

- Recipe can be prepared a day ahead.
- Storage: Covered, in refrigerator.
- Freeze: Not suitable.
- Microwave: Not suitable.

PAN-FRIED POTATOES

3 medium (about 450g) potatoes
2 tablespoons olive oil
20g butter
1 tablespoon chopped fresh rosemary
1 teaspoon celery salt

Cut potatoes into 2cm cubes. Boil, steam or microwave until just tender; drain.

Heat oil and butter in pan, add potatoes, rosemary and salt. Cook, stirring occasionally, until potatoes are browned and crisp; drain on absorbent paper.

- Recipe best made just before serving.
- Freeze: Not suitable.
- Microwave: Potatoes suitable to boil.

ROCKET AND RADICCHIO SALAD

½ small radicchio lettuce
8 rocket lettuce leaves
½ small butter lettuce
¼ red pepper, thinly sliced
4 cherry tomatoes, halved

DRESSING
¼ cup olive oil
1 tablespoon red wine vinegar
½ teaspoon seeded mustard
pinch sugar
¼ teaspoon ground black
    peppercorns

Tear lettuce leaves into pieces, combine with remaining ingredients in bowl, drizzle with dressing.

Dressing: Combine all ingredients in jar; shake well.

- Recipe best made just before serving.
- Freeze: Not suitable.

LEFT: Chicken with Olives and Prunes, Pan-Fried Potatoes and Rocket and Radicchio Salad.

China from Corso de Fiori.

SEAFOOD

You don't need heaps of ingredients to make seafood as wonderfully different as the salmon fillets on our cover or the honeyed lobster at right, both a dream to eat. Even quicker is superb grilled tuna or our refreshing prawn and cucumber salad. Other tasty treats include a spicy fish stew with nutty rice, and tuna and squid kebabs with polenta. Every main recipe, of course, has its own delicious accompaniments.

Lobster with Avocado Sauce

Goats' Cheese and Carambola Salad

LOBSTER WITH AVOCADO SAUCE

2 small (about 450g) uncooked lobster tails
2 tablespoons dry white wine
1 tablespoon honey
1 teaspoon chopped fresh red chillies
1 clove garlic, crushed
1 tablespoon oil
20g butter

AVOCADO SAUCE
½ small avocado
2 tablespoons oil
1 tablespoon lime juice
1 tablespoon cream
¼ teaspoon sugar

Remove flesh from lobster tails. Place flesh in shallow dish, pour over combined wine, honey, chilli and garlic, cover, refrigerate several hours or overnight.

Drain lobster from marinade, reserve marinade. Heat oil and butter in pan, add lobster, cook until browned all over.

Transfer to oven tray, brush with reserved marinade. Bake lobster, uncovered, in moderate oven about 10 minutes or until just tender. Slice thickly, serve with avocado sauce.

Avocado Sauce: Blend all ingredients until smooth.

- Lobster can be prepared a day ahead. Sauce best made just before serving.
- Storage: Lobster, covered, in refrigerator.
- Freeze: Not suitable.
- Microwave: Not suitable.

GOATS' CHEESE AND CARAMBOLA SALAD

60g goats' cheese
½ rocket lettuce
½ red oak leaf lettuce
2 small carambolas, sliced

DRESSING
2 tablespoons olive oil
2 teaspoons balsamic vinegar
2 teaspoons lemon juice
1 teaspoon fresh thyme leaves
pinch sugar

Cut cheese into wedges; tear lettuce into pieces. Place cheese, lettuce and carambolas on plates; add dressing.

Dressing: Combine all ingredients in jar; shake well.

- Can be prepared 3 hours ahead.
- Storage: Salad and dressing separately, covered, in refrigerator.
- Freeze: Not suitable.

RIGHT: Lobster with Avocado Sauce and Goats' Cheese and Carambola Salad.

Bowl from Bibelot; servers from The Bay Tree; tiles from Pazotti.

Fish Parcels with Mint Seasoning

Squash and Asparagus in Saffron Butter

FISH PARCELS WITH MINT SEASONING

4 sheets fillo pastry
40g butter, melted
2 white fish fillets

MINT SEASONING
⅓ cup coconut cream
pinch turmeric
1 teaspoon ground cumin
¼ teaspoon sambal oelek
1 teaspoon mango chutney
2 tablespoons chopped fresh mint
1 tablespoon chopped fresh coriander
1 tablespoon chopped fresh lemon grass
1 clove garlic, crushed

Layer 2 pastry sheets together, brushing each with butter. Place a fish fillet at a short end, spread fish with mint seasoning, roll pastry, folding in ends to form a parcel. Brush with butter, place on greased oven tray. Repeat with remaining pastry, butter, fish and mint seasoning. Bake parcels, uncovered, in hot oven about 15 minutes or until pastry is browned and fish is cooked through. Serve with squash and asparagus in saffron butter.
Mint Seasoning: Blend or process all ingredients until combined.

■ Recipe best made just before serving.
■ Freeze: Not suitable.
■ Microwave: Not suitable.

SQUASH AND ASPARAGUS IN SAFFRON BUTTER

½ bunch (6 spears) fresh asparagus
10 baby yellow squash, halved
40g butter
pinch ground saffron
1 tablespoon chopped fresh chives
1 tablespoon chopped fresh parsley

Cut asparagus into 4cm pieces. Boil, steam or microwave asparagus and squash until just tender. Heat butter in pan, add vegetables and saffron, stir-fry until heated through; stir in herbs.

■ Vegetables can be prepared 3 hours ahead.
■ Storage: Covered, in refrigerator.
■ Freeze: Not suitable.
■ Microwave: Suitable.

Spicy Fish Stew

Nutty Rice

SPICY FISH STEW

2 (about 650g) firm white thick fish
cutlets or fillets
1 tablespoon turmeric
2 tablespoons oil
½ onion, chopped
¼ teaspoon chilli powder
¼ teaspoon ground coriander
¼ teaspoon ground cumin
¼ teaspoon garam marsala
410g can tomatoes
⅓ cup tomato puree
2 tablespoons sour cream
1 tablespoon chopped fresh
coriander

Cut fish into 3cm cubes; toss fish in turmeric. Heat oil in pan, add fish; cook until lightly browned; remove from pan. Add onion and spices to pan, cook, stirring, until onion is soft. Stir in undrained crushed tomatoes and puree, simmer, uncovered, about 2 minutes or until slightly thickened. Stir in fish; cook, uncovered, until fish is tender; remove from heat, stir in sour cream and fresh coriander. Serve with nutty rice.

■ Recipe best made just before serving.
■ Freeze: Not suitable.
■ Microwave: Not suitable.

NUTTY RICE

¾ cup white rice
1 tablespoon oil
¼ cup sultanas
½ cup unsalted roasted cashews
1 tablespoon chopped fresh
coriander
1 tablespoon chopped fresh parsley

Add rice to large pan of boiling water, boil, uncovered, until just tender, rinse under cold water; drain. Heat oil in pan, add rice, stir in remaining ingredients, stir over heat until heated through.

■ Recipe can be made a day ahead.
■ Freeze: Suitable.
■ Microwave: Suitable.

FAR LEFT: Fish Parcels with Mint Seasoning and Squash and Asparagus in Saffron Butter. LEFT: Spicy Fish Stew with Nutty Rice.

Far left: Cutlery, place mat and serviette from Country Road Homewares; salt and pepper set from Bibelot. Left: Plate, bowls, cutlery and serviette from The Bay Tree; tiles from Pazotti.

Baked Trout with Onion and Artichokes

Potato and Prosciutto Salad

BAKED TROUT WITH ONION AND ARTICHOKES

2 rainbow trout
6 artichoke hearts, drained, halved
1 small red Spanish onion, sliced
½ teaspoon chopped fresh coriander
½ teaspoon chopped fresh dill
1 tablespoon lemon juice
20g butter, chopped
¼ teaspoon ground black peppercorns

Place each fish in centre of piece of greased foil. Sprinkle fish with remaining ingredients. Fold foil around fish to form parcels, seal edges firmly; place parcels on oven tray. Bake in moderate oven about 25 minutes or until fish are tender. Serve with potato and prosciutto salad.

- Recipe best made just before serving.
- Freeze: Not suitable.
- Microwave: Not suitable.

POTATO AND PROSCIUTTO SALAD

250g baby potatoes
50g sliced prosciutto

DRESSING
2 green shallots, chopped
2 teaspoons lemon juice
1 tablespoon olive oil

Boil, steam or microwave potatoes until just tender; drain. Slice prosciutto into

1cm strips. Combine potatoes and prosciutto in bowl, pour over dressing.
Dressing: Combine all ingredients in jar; shake well.

- ▣ Recipe can be prepared 6 hours ahead.
- ▣ Storage: Covered, in refrigerator.
- ▣ Freeze: Not suitable.
- ▣ Microwave: Potatoes suitable.

BELOW: Baked Trout with Onion and Artichokes and Potato and Prosciutto Salad.

Below: Salad bowl, cutlery and ladle from Jarass; serviette ring from Accoutrement.

Fish with Mushroom Prosciutto Sauce

Herbed Lemon and Zucchini Spirals

FISH WITH MUSHROOM PROSCIUTTO SAUCE

1 tablespoon olive oil
½ teaspoon paprika
½ teaspoon cracked black
  peppercorns
2 firm white fish cutlets

MUSHROOM PROSCIUTTO SAUCE
50g thinly sliced prosciutto
15g butter
50g oyster mushrooms, halved
50g baby mushrooms, sliced
2 tablespoons dry white wine
¾ cup cream

Combine oil, paprika and peppercorns in bowl. Brush fish with oil mixture. Cook fish in hot pan until tender. Serve with mushroom prosciutto sauce, and herbed lemon and zucchini spirals.
Mushroom Prosciutto Sauce: Cut prosciutto into 1cm strips. Heat butter in pan, add prosciutto, cook, stirring, until crisp. Add mushrooms, cook, stirring, until soft. Stir in wine and cream, simmer, uncovered, about 5 minutes or until thickened.

- ▣ Mushroom prosciutto sauce can be made 3 hours ahead.
- ▣ Storage: Covered, in refrigerator.
- ▣ Freeze: Not suitable.
- ▣ Microwave: Sauce suitable.

HERBED LEMON AND ZUCCHINI SPIRALS

100g spiral pasta
2 small (about 130g) zucchini
½ bunch (6 spears) fresh asparagus
2 tablespoons olive oil
1 clove garlic, crushed
1 small onion, sliced
1 tablespoon lemon juice
1 teaspoon chopped fresh
  lemon thyme

Add pasta to pan of boiling water, boil, uncovered, until just tender, drain.

Cut zucchini into 5cm strips. Cut asparagus into 5cm lengths. Heat oil in pan, add garlic and onion, cook, stirring, until onion is soft. Add zucchini, asparagus and juice, cook, stirring, until vegetables are tender. Add thyme and pasta, stir until heated through.

- ▣ Recipe can be made 3 hours ahead.
- ▣ Storage: Covered, in refrigerator.
- ▣ Freeze: Not suitable.
- ▣ Microwave: Suitable.

ABOVE: Fish with Mushroom Prosciutto Sauce and Herbed Lemon and Zucchini Spirals.

Above: Plate from Horgan Imports; cutlery from Jarass; mats from Piper Bishop.

Tuna and Squid Kebabs with Polenta

Green Salad with Garlic Dressing

TUNA AND SQUID KEBABS WITH POLENTA

350g tuna steak
150g squid hoods
2 tablespoons olive oil
1 tablespoon balsamic vinegar
⅓ cup lemon juice
½ cup shredded fresh basil
½ teaspoon garlic salt

POLENTA
2 cups water
⅔ cup polenta
⅓ cup grated parmesan cheese
20g butter

TOMATO SAUCE
1 tablespoon olive oil
1 onion, sliced
1 clove garlic, crushed
410g can tomatoes
1 tablespoon shredded fresh basil

Cut tuna into 3cm cubes; cut squid hoods into 3cm strips.

Combine oil, vinegar, juice, basil and salt in bowl, add tuna and squid; mix well, cover, refrigerate 3 hours or overnight.

Drain seafood, reserve marinade. Thread tuna and squid onto 4 skewers. Grill kebabs until tender, brushing occasionally with reserved marinade. Serve kebabs with polenta and tomato sauce, and green salad with garlic dressing.

Polenta: Grease 8cm x 26cm bar cake pan. Bring water to boil in pan, stir in polenta, simmer, covered, about 30 minutes, stirring occasionally, until mixture is thickened. Remove from heat, stir in cheese and butter. Spread mixture into prepared pan. Bake, uncovered, in hot oven, about 10 minutes or until heated through. Cut into desired shapes.

Tomato Sauce: Heat oil in pan, add onion and garlic, cook, stirring, until onion is soft. Add undrained crushed tomatoes, simmer, uncovered, about 10 minutes or until thickened slightly; stir in basil.

■ Polenta and tomato sauce can be prepared 3 hours ahead.
■ Storage: Covered, in refrigerator.
■ Freeze: Not suitable.
■ Microwave: Tomato sauce suitable.

LEFT: Tuna and Squid Kebabs with Polenta and Green Salad with Garlic Dressing. ABOVE: Prawn and Cucumber Salad.

Left: Salad bowl, jug and cutlery from Jarass; napery from Piper Bishop; glasses from Mosmania; serviette ring from Accoutrement. Above: Plates from Horgan Imports; cutlery and salad servers from Jarass; glasses from Mosmania; serviettes and mats from Piper Bishop; serviette rings from Accoutrement.

Prawn and Cucumber Salad

GREEN SALAD WITH GARLIC DRESSING

3 cos lettuce leaves
4 mignonette lettuce leaves
2 radicchio lettuce leaves
6 cherry tomatoes, halved

GARLIC DRESSING
½ teaspoon French mustard
½ teaspoon sugar
¼ cup olive oil
2 teaspoons white wine vinegar
2 cloves garlic, crushed
¼ teaspoon seasoned pepper

Combine torn lettuce and tomatoes in bowl, drizzle with garlic dressing.

Garlic Dressing: Combine all ingredients in jar; shake well.

■ Recipe best made just before serving.
■ Freeze: Not suitable.

PRAWN AND CUCUMBER SALAD

500g cooked prawns
1 small green cucumber
250g packet Japanese dried noodles
2 teaspoons sesame oil
1 cup (100g) bean sprouts
1 cup shredded red cabbage
2 green shallots, chopped
1 tablespoon thinly sliced Japanese pickled pink ginger

WASABI DRESSING
2 tablespoons rice vinegar
1 teaspoon fish sauce
1 teaspoon light soy sauce
¼ teaspoon wasabi paste or powder
1 tablespoon oil

Shell and devein prawns, leaving tails intact. Slice cucumber lengthways into very thin slices.

Add noodles to large pan of boiling water, boil, uncovered, until just tender; drain. Place noodles in bowl, toss with sesame oil. Add prawns, cucumber, bean sprouts, cabbage, shallots and ginger; mix well, drizzle with wasabi dressing.

Wasabi Dressing: Combine all ingredients in jar; shake well.

■ Recipe best made just before serving.
■ Freeze: Not suitable.
■ Microwave: Noodles suitable.

Warm Fish Salad

Onion Pinwheels

WARM FISH SALAD

½ bunch (6 spears) fresh
    asparagus, sliced
50g green beans, sliced
50g snow peas
1 small mignonette lettuce
¼ cup fresh flat-leafed parsley sprigs
8 cherry tomatoes, halved
2 tablespoons oil
20g butter
350g piece firm white fish,
    thinly sliced

VINAIGRETTE
¼ cup lemon juice
¼ cup olive oil
½ teaspoon French mustard
½ teaspoon sugar

Boil, steam or microwave asparagus, beans and peas until just tender; rinse under cold water, drain. Combine vegetables, torn lettuce leaves, parsley and tomatoes on serving plates.

Heat oil and butter in pan, add fish; cook until tender. Serve fish with salad, drizzle with warm vinaigrette. Serve with onion pinwheels.

Vinaigrette: Combine all ingredients in pan; bring to boil; whisk until combined.

■ Recipe best made just before serving.
■ Freeze: Not suitable.
■ Microwave: Vegetables suitable.

ONION PINWHEELS

2 tablespoons oil
2 medium (about 300g) onions, sliced
1 tablespoon brown sugar
2 teaspoons balsamic vinegar
1 cup self-raising flour
20g butter
¼ cup milk, approximately

Heat oil in pan, add onions, cook, stirring occasionally, over low heat until onions are very soft. Stir in sugar and vinegar, cook, stirring, about 3 minutes or until onions are caramel in colour; drain on absorbent paper, cool.

Sift flour into bowl, rub in butter, stir in enough milk to mix to a soft dough; knead dough lightly on floured surface until smooth. Roll dough to 15cm x 25cm rectangle; spread onion mixture over dough. Roll up firmly from short side; trim edges. Cover roll, refrigerate 30 minutes.

Cut roll into 8 slices, place slices on greased oven tray; bake in moderately hot oven about 15 minutes or until pinwheels are cooked through.

■ Recipe can be made a day ahead.
■ Storage: Airtight container.
■ Freeze: Suitable.
■ Microwave: Not suitable.

LEFT: Warm Fish Salad with Onion Pinwheels.

Plate and bowl, glass and ginger grater from Mosmania; serviettes from Piper Bishop.

Grilled Tuna with Tomato Vinaigrette

Roast Potatoes and Peppers

GRILLED TUNA WITH TOMATO VINAIGRETTE

2 medium tuna steaks
20g butter, melted

TOMATO VINAIGRETTE
2½ tablespoons olive oil
2 teaspoons balsamic vinegar
2 green shallots, chopped
2 teaspoons drained chopped
    sun-dried tomatoes
2 teaspoons water

Grill or barbecue tuna steaks until just tender, brushing with butter during cooking. Serve with tomato vinaigrette and roast potatoes and peppers.
Tomato Vinaigrette: Combine all ingredients in jar; shake well.

■ Tuna best cooked just before serving. Vinaigrette can be made a day ahead.
■ Storage: Vinaigrette, covered, in refrigerator.
■ Freeze: Not suitable.
■ Microwave: Not suitable.

ROAST POTATOES AND PEPPERS

1 tablespoon olive oil
250g chat potatoes, quartered
½ red pepper, thinly sliced
½ green pepper, thinly sliced
1 onion, sliced
2 cloves garlic, crushed

Heat oil in baking dish, stir in remaining ingredients. Bake, uncovered, in hot oven about 30 minutes, stirring occasionally, or until potatoes are tender.

■ Recipe best made just before serving.
■ Freeze: Not suitable.
■ Microwave: Not suitable.

BELOW: Grilled Tuna with Tomato Vinaigrette and Roast Potatoes and Peppers.

Plates from Accoutrement; cutlery from Jarass; mats from Piper Bishop.

LEMON PEPPER GRILLED FISH

1 lemon
1 (about 700g) whole firm white fish
2 tablespoons lemon juice
2 teaspoons oyster sauce
2 tablespoons olive oil
1 teaspoon seasoned pepper
1 clove garlic, crushed
1/2 teaspoon sugar
2 teaspoons chopped fresh mint
1/4 red pepper, finely chopped

Using vegetable peeler, peel lemon rind very thinly, cut rind into thin strips; you need 1 tablespoon rind.

Make 3 cuts on each side of fish. Combine the 1 tablespoon rind, juice, sauce, oil, seasoned pepper, garlic, sugar, mint and red pepper in bowl; mix well. Rub pepper mixture into both sides of fish, cover, refrigerate 2 hours.

Drain fish from marinade, reserve marinade. Place fish on wire rack in flameproof dish, grill until browned and tender. Heat reserved marinade in pan, bring to boil, remove from heat, pour over fish. Serve with risoni and wild rice salad.

- Recipe can be prepared 3 hours ahead.
- Storage: Covered, in refrigerator.
- Freeze: Not suitable
- Microwave: Not suitable.

RISONI AND WILD RICE SALAD

1/4 cup risoni
1/4 cup wild rice
2 teaspoons oil
4 green shallots, chopped
3 teaspoons chopped fresh
   lemon grass
1 teaspoon lime juice
1/4 teaspoon fish sauce
30g butter

Add risoni to pan of boiling water, boil, uncovered, until tender; drain. Add rice to pan of boiling water, boil, uncovered, about 40 minutes or until tender; drain.

Heat oil in pan, add shallots and lemon grass, cook, stirring, until shallots are soft. Add risoni, rice, juice and sauce, stir until heated through; transfer to serving dish.

Add butter to same pan, cook until butter is lightly browned, pour over rice mixture; mix gently.

- Risoni and rice can be cooked a day ahead.
- Storage: Covered, in refrigerator.
- Freeze: Not suitable.
- Microwave: Risoni and rice suitable.

Lemon Pepper Grilled Fish

Risoni and Wild Rice Salad

LEFT: Lemon Pepper Grilled Fish with Risoni and Wild Rice Salad.

Blue and white plate from Butler & Co., silver plate from Home & Garden; napery from Country Road Homewares; servers from Thip Thai Restaurant.

Spaghetti with Tuna and Pepper Sauce

Olive and Onion Salad

SPAGHETTI WITH TUNA AND PEPPER SAUCE

200g spaghetti pasta
1 tablespoon olive oil
½ green pepper, thinly sliced
1 small onion, sliced
400g can tomatoes
1 zucchini, chopped
1 teaspoon sugar
185g can tuna, drained
2 tablespoons chopped fresh basil
2 tablespoons coarsely grated
 parmesan cheese

Add pasta to large pan of boiling water, boil, uncovered, until just tender; drain.

Heat oil in pan, add pepper and onion, cook, stirring, until vegetables are tender. Stir in undrained crushed tomatoes, zucchini and sugar, simmer, uncovered, until zucchini is just tender. Add tuna and basil, stir gently until heated through. Serve sauce with pasta, sprinkle with cheese. Serve with olive and onion salad.

■ Recipe best made just before serving.
■ Freeze: Not suitable.
■ Microwave: Suitable.

OLIVE AND ONION SALAD

½ butter lettuce
½ small green cucumber, sliced
8 cherry tomatoes, halved
¼ cup black olives, halved
1 small red Spanish onion, sliced
⅓ cup Italian dressing

Tear lettuce into pieces, combine in bowl with cucumber, tomatoes, olives and onion; drizzle with dressing.

■ Recipe best made just before serving.
■ Freeze: Not suitable.

LEFT: Spaghetti with Tuna and Pepper Sauce and Olive and Onion Salad.
RIGHT: Salmon with Spinach and Lime Butter Sauce and Peppered Potatoes.

Left: China by Taitu from David Jones, Sydney; cutlery from Paraphernalia; serviette and salad bowl from Home & Garden; salt and pepper set from Georg Jensen. Right: China with salmon, and salt and pepper set from Wedgwood; Christofle cutlery from David Jones, Sydney; wine glass and gold-rimmed china from Noritake; salt dish from Lindfield Antique Centre.

Salmon with Spinach and Lime Butter Sauce

Peppered Potatoes

SALMON WITH SPINACH AND LIME BUTTER SAUCE

2 salmon fillets
1 bunch (40 leaves) English spinach
20g butter
1 clove garlic, crushed

LIME BUTTER SAUCE
2 tablespoons lime juice
½ cup cream
40g butter, chopped
1 tablespoon chopped fresh chives

Grill fish until cooked through. Add spinach to large pan of boiling water, drain; rinse under cold water, drain well.

Heat butter and garlic in pan, add spinach, cook, stirring, until spinach is heated through.

Divide spinach between 2 serving plates, top with fish, spoon over lime butter sauce. Serve with peppered potatoes.

Lime Butter Sauce: Simmer juice in pan until reduced by half. Add cream, stir over heat, without boiling, 1 minute, quickly whisk in butter; stir in chives.

- Recipe best made just before serving.
- Freeze: Not suitable.
- Microwave: Spinach suitable.

PEPPERED POTATOES

1 tablespoon olive oil
250g small potatoes, halved
½ teaspoon cracked black
   peppercorns
pinch paprika

Heat oil in baking dish, add potatoes, toss in oil until coated. Sprinkle potatoes with peppercorns and paprika, bake, uncovered, in moderately hot oven about 30 minutes or until tender.

- Recipe best made just before serving.
- Freeze: Not suitable.
- Microwave: Not suitable.

Baked Fish with Tahini Sauce

Deep-Fried Onion Rings

Steamed Beans

BAKED FISH WITH TAHINI SAUCE

⅓ **cup lime juice**
¼ **cup fresh flat-leafed parsley sprigs**
¼ **cup chopped fresh coriander**
1 **tablespoon chopped fresh
    lemon grass**
½ **teaspoon cracked black
    peppercorns**
2 **small whole snapper**
½ **cup dry white wine**
½ **cup water**

TAHINI SAUCE
½ **cup tahini paste**
1 **clove garlic, crushed**
½ **cup warm water**
¼ **cup lime juice**
2 **tablespoons chopped fresh
    coriander**
2 **tablespoons chopped fresh
    flat-leafed parsley**

Combine juice, herbs, lemon grass and peppercorns in bowl, fill fish with herb mixture. Transfer fish to greased baking dish, pour over combined wine and water, cover dish with foil. Bake in moderately hot oven about 25 minutes or until fish are tender. Serve with tahini sauce, steamed beans and deep-fried onion rings.
Tahini Sauce: Blend or process paste and garlic, gradually add water and juice while motor is operating; stir in herbs.

- ■ Fish best cooked just before serving. Sauce can be made a day ahead.
- ■ Storage: Sauce, covered, in refrigerator.
- ■ Freeze: Not suitable.
- ■ Microwave: Suitable.

DEEP-FRIED ONION RINGS

1 **onion**
⅓ **cup plain flour**
1 **teaspoon garlic salt**
⅓ **cup mineral water**
oil for deep-frying

Cut onion into 1cm slices, separate slices into rings. Sift flour into bowl, add salt, whisk in water. Dip rings in batter, deep-fry in hot oil until browned and crisp; drain on absorbent paper.

- ■ Recipe best made just before serving.
- ■ Freeze: Not suitable.
- ■ Microwave: Not suitable.

STEAMED BEANS

125g **green beans**
125g **yellow beans**
15g **butter**

Cut beans into 6cm lengths. Boil, steam or microwave beans until just tender, rinse under cold water; drain. Return beans to pan, add butter, stir over heat until hot.

- ■ Recipe best made just before serving.
- ■ Freeze: Not suitable.
- ■ Microwave: Suitable.

Potato-Topped Salmon Mornay

Salad with Lemon Dressing

POTATO-TOPPED SALMON MORNAY

30g butter
1 onion, chopped
1 stick celery, chopped
1 tablespoon plain flour
¾ cup milk
⅓ cup cream
⅓ cup grated tasty cheese
210g can salmon, drained, flaked
2 tablespoons chopped dill pickles
**2 tablespoons grated tasty
   cheese, extra**

POTATO TOPPING
2 large (about 400g) potatoes
1 tablespoon milk
20g butter
2 teaspoons chopped fresh chives

Heat butter in pan, add onion and celery, cook, stirring, until onion is soft. Add flour, stir 1 minute or until mixture is bubbly. Remove from heat, gradually stir in combined milk and cream, stir over heat until mixture boils and thickens. Remove from heat, stir in cheese, salmon and pickles.

Spoon mixture into 2 ovenproof dishes (1⅓ cup capacity). Spread potato topping over salmon mixture, sprinkle with extra cheese. Bake, uncovered, in moderately hot oven about 25 minutes or until hot. Serve with salad with lemon dressing.

Potato Topping: Boil, steam or microwave potatoes until tender; drain. Mash potatoes with milk and butter until smooth, stir in chives.

- Recipe can be made a day ahead.
- Storage: Covered, in refrigerator.
- Freeze: Not suitable.
- Microwave: Suitable.

SALAD WITH LEMON DRESSING

½ small red pepper
4 mignonette lettuce leaves
4 butter lettuce leaves
½ cup alfalfa sprouts
50g baby mushrooms, sliced

LEMON DRESSING
¼ cup oil
1 teaspoon grated lemon rind
1 tablespoon lemon juice
1 clove garlic, crushed
pinch cracked black peppercorns

Cut pepper into thin rings. Combine all ingredients in bowl, add lemon dressing; mix gently.

Lemon Dressing: Combine all ingredients in jar, shake well.

- Salad best made just before serving. Lemon dressing can be made a day ahead.
- Storage: Covered, in refrigerator.
- Freeze: Not suitable.

LEFT: Baked Fish with Tahini Sauce, Deep-Fried Onion Rings and Steamed Beans. ABOVE: Potato-Topped Salmon Mornay and Salad with Lemon Dressing.

Left: China from Noritake at David Jones, Sydney; Alessi bowl from Paraphernalia; napery from Country Road Homewares.

CRISP PAN-FRIED FISH WITH ANCHOVY BUTTER

4 small fish fillets
plain flour
1 egg, lightly beaten
2 tablespoons cream
2 tablespoons oil

ANCHOVY BUTTER
50g soft butter
3 anchovy fillets, drained
1 clove garlic, crushed
2 teaspoons chopped fresh basil

Toss fish in flour, shake away excess flour, dip fish in combined egg and cream.

Heat oil in pan, add fish, cook until browned and crisp; drain on absorbent paper. Serve with anchovy butter and green salad, if desired. Serve with shoestring potatoes.

Anchovy Butter: Combine butter, anchovies, garlic and basil in bowl; mix well. Spoon mixture onto foil, shape into a log, roll up firmly. Refrigerate until firm.

- Butter can be made a day ahead.
- Storage: Covered, in refrigerator.
- Freeze: Butter suitable.
- Microwave: Not suitable.

SHOESTRING POTATOES

2 medium (about 300g) potatoes, peeled
oil for deep-frying

Slice potatoes very thinly into 2mm slices, slice into 2mm strips. Cover potatoes with water in bowl; stand 2 hours.

Drain potatoes; pat dry with absorbent paper; deep-fry in hot oil until crisp and golden; drain on absorbent paper.

- Recipe must be prepared 2 hours ahead.
- Storage: Potatoes, covered with water, at room temperature.
- Freeze: Not suitable.
- Microwave: Not suitable.

RIGHT: Crisp Pan-Fried Fish with Anchovy Butter and Shoestring Potatoes.

Crisp Pan-Fried Fish with Anchovy Butter

Shoestring Potatoes

Beef

Tender steak and fillets dressed with garlic ginger carrots, spiced honey sauce, redcurrant

sauce or olive and anchovy dressing give you an idea of the tempting recipes in this

section. For a more casual occasion, there is beef and mushroom ragout, satay beef

spare ribs, tasty braised meatballs, beef and caper burgers and two terrific salads.

Of the accompaniments, you'll be specially intrigued by turnip puree in pastry shells

and mushroom and pepper timbales.

Beef, Noodle and Vegetable Salad

BEEF, NOODLE AND VEGETABLE SALAD

1 tablespoon oil
300g piece beef eye-fillet steak
100g rice vermicelli
½ bunch (about 6 spears) fresh asparagus
1 carrot
50g snow peas
½ red pepper, thinly sliced
1 small onion, sliced
½ bunch (20 leaves) English spinach
1 cup (80g) bean sprouts

DRESSING
¼ cup lime juice
2 tablespoons oil
1 tablespoon chopped fresh lemon grass
1 tablespoon chopped fresh coriander
2 teaspoons fish sauce
2 teaspoons sugar
1 clove garlic, crushed
1 small fresh red chilli, finely chopped

Heat oil in pan, add steak, cook until done as desired; cool. Slice steak thinly, combine with half the dressing in bowl, cover, refrigerate several hours.

Add vermicelli to pan of boiling water, boil, uncovered, until tender; drain, cool.

Cut asparagus into 7cm lengths. Cut carrot into long thin strips. Add asparagus, carrot, peas and pepper to pan of boiling water, drain immediately; rinse under cold water, drain well. Combine all vegetables in bowl, toss well. Place vegetables on serving plates, top with vermicelli and steak. Drizzle with remaining dressing.

Dressing: Combine all ingredients in jar; shake well.

■ Recipe can be prepared 3 hours ahead.
■ Storage: Covered, in refrigerator.
■ Freeze: Not suitable.
■ Microwave: Vegetables suitable.

RIGHT: Beef, Noodle and Vegetable Salad.

China and cutlery from Limoges.

Steak with Olive and Anchovy Dressing

Three Pepper Saute

Garlic Potatoes

STEAK WITH OLIVE AND ANCHOVY DRESSING

1 tablespoon oil
2 scotch fillet steaks

OLIVE AND ANCHOVY DRESSING
1 teaspoon drained capers, chopped
1 anchovy fillet, chopped
2 tablespoons chopped fresh
**   flat-leafed parsley**
2 teaspoons lemon juice
1 tablespoon olive oil
6 black olives, finely chopped

Heat oil in pan, add steaks, cook until done as desired. Serve steaks with olive and anchovy dressing. Serve with three pepper saute and garlic potatoes.
Olive and Anchovy Dressing: Combine all ingredients in bowl; mix well.

- Steaks best cooked just before serving. Olive and anchovy dressing can be made a day ahead.
- Storage: Covered, in refrigerator.
- Freeze: Not suitable.
- Microwave: Not suitable.

THREE PEPPER SAUTE

½ red pepper
½ green pepper
½ yellow pepper
30g butter
1 clove garlic, crushed

Cut peppers into strips. Heat butter in pan, add peppers and garlic, cook, stirring, until peppers are tender.

- Recipe best made just before serving.
- Freeze: Not suitable.
- Microwave: Suitable.

GARLIC POTATOES

4 small (about 180g) potatoes
½ teaspoon garlic salt
⅓ cup cream

Grease 2 ovenproof dishes (½ cup capacity). Slice potatoes thinly; sprinkle with garlic salt. Place potatoes in prepared dishes; pour over cream. Bake, uncovered, in moderate oven about 45 minutes or until potatoes are tender. Sprinkle with paprika, if desired.

- Recipe can be made a day ahead.
- Storage: Covered, in refrigerator.
- Freeze: Not suitable.
- Microwave: Suitable.

LEFT: Steak with Olive and Anchovy Dressing, Three Pepper Saute and Garlic Potatoes.

China from Villeroy & Boch.

Beef and Mushroom Ragout

Baked Kumara Crescents

BEEF AND MUSHROOM RAGOUT

600g chuck steak
1 tablespoon olive oil
1 onion, chopped
1 clove garlic, crushed
2 sticks celery, chopped
½ cup dry red wine
2 cups beef stock
2 tablespoons tomato paste
½ teaspoon seasoned pepper
4 chat potatoes, quartered
100g baby mushrooms
1 zucchini, chopped

Cut steak into 3cm cubes. Heat oil in pan, add steak in batches, cook, stirring, until well browned all over; remove from pan. Add onion, garlic and celery to same pan, cook, stirring, until onion is soft.

Return steak to pan, stir in wine, stock, paste and pepper, simmer, covered, 1 hour, stirring occasionally. Add potatoes, simmer, covered, further 15 minutes. Stir in mushrooms and zucchini, simmer, uncovered, further 15 minutes or until steak and vegetables are tender. Serve with baked kumara crescents.

■ Recipe can be made a day ahead.
■ Storage: Covered, in refrigerator.
■ Freeze: Suitable.
■ Microwave: Not suitable.

BAKED KUMARA CRESCENTS

300g kumara, peeled
plain flour
¼ teaspoon paprika
¼ teaspoon garlic salt
¼ teaspoon dried rosemary leaves
¼ teaspoon dried oregano leaves
20g butter, melted

Cut kumara into 3 thick slices, cut each slice in half to form crescents. Toss crescents in flour, shake away excess flour. Place crescents on greased oven tray, sprinkle with combined paprika, salt and herbs, drizzle with butter. Bake, uncovered, in moderately hot oven about 30 minutes or until kumara crescents are soft and browned.

■ Recipe best made just before serving.
■ Freeze: Not suitable.
■ Microwave: Not suitable.

ABOVE: Beef and Mushroom Ragout with Baked Kumara Crescents.

China and cutlery from Limoges.

Fillet of Beef with Redcurrant Sauce

Turnip Puree in Pastry Shells

Spinach Salad with Berry Dressing

FILLET OF BEEF WITH REDCURRRANT SAUCE

2 tablespoons oil
400g piece beef eye-fillet steak

REDCURRANT SAUCE
20g butter
1 onion, finely chopped
2 cloves garlic, crushed
80g baby mushrooms, sliced
3 teaspoons drained green peppercorns
1/3 cup dry red wine
2 tablespoons redcurrant jelly
1/4 teaspoon beef stock powder
1 tablespoon port
20g butter, extra

Heat oil in flameproof dish, add steak, cook over high heat until well browned all over. Bake, uncovered, in hot oven about 10 minutes or until steak is tender and done as desired. Serve with redcurrant sauce, turnip puree in pastry shells and spinach salad with berry dressing.
Redcurrant Sauce: Heat butter in pan, add onion, garlic and mushrooms, cook, stirring, until onion is soft. Add peppercorns and wine, simmer, uncovered, 1 minute. Stir in jelly, stock powder and port, simmer further 4 minutes or until slightly thickened. Quickly whisk in extra butter over low heat.

- Recipe best made just before serving.
- Freeze: Not suitable.
- Microwave: Sauce suitable.

TURNIP PUREE IN PASTRY SHELLS

2/3 cup plain flour
30g butter
2 tablespoons water, approximately

TURNIP PUREE
1 medium (about 300g) swede turnip, chopped
1 tablespoon dry sherry
2 teaspoons chopped fresh parsley

Grease 2 moulds (1/2 cup capacity). Sift flour into bowl, rub in butter, add enough water to make ingredients cling together. Press dough into ball, knead gently on floured surface until smooth; cover; refrigerate 30 minutes.

Roll dough on floured surface large enough to line prepared moulds, trim edges. Line pastry with paper, fill with dried beans or rice. Bake in moderately hot oven about 10 minutes, remove paper and beans, bake further 10 minutes or until pastry is browned. Serve pastry shells filled with turnip puree.
Turnip Puree: Boil, steam or microwave turnip until tender; drain well. Blend or process turnip and sherry until smooth; stir in parsley.

- Pastry shells can be made 2 days ahead. Turnip puree best made just before serving.
- Storage: Pastry shells in airtight container at room temperature.
- Freeze: Not suitable.
- Microwave: Turnip suitable.

SPINACH SALAD WITH BERRY DRESSING

12 leaves English spinach
2 green shallots, finely chopped
50g snow peas, chopped

BERRY DRESSING
1/2 cup strawberries
1 teaspoon balsamic vinegar
2 teaspoons olive oil
1/2 teaspoon redcurrant jelly

Combine torn spinach leaves, shallots and snow peas in bowl; drizzle with berry dressing; toss gently.
Berry Dressing: Blend or process all ingredients until smooth; strain. Or, push ingredients through fine sieve.

- Recipe best made just before serving.
- Freeze: Not suitable.

LEFT: Fillet of Beef with Redcurrant Sauce, Turnip Puree in Pastry Shells and Spinach Salad with Berry Dressing.

China from Noritake.

Steak with Garlic Ginger Carrots

Braised Chinese Broccoli

Deep-Fried Crispy Noodles

STEAK WITH GARLIC GINGER CARROTS

2 medium rump steaks
1 tablespoon dark soy sauce
¼ teaspoon sesame oil
1 tablespoon oil

GARLIC GINGER CARROTS
2 tablespoons oil
2 cloves garlic, crushed
1 tablespoon grated fresh ginger
2 (about 240g) carrots, chopped
2 green shallots, sliced
⅓ cup dry white wine
¼ cup water
pinch chilli flakes
2 teaspoons chopped fresh oregano

Combine steaks, sauce and sesame oil in bowl, cover, refrigerate 3 hours or overnight.

Heat oil in pan, add steaks, cook until tender and done as desired; drain on absorbent paper. Slice steaks, serve topped with garlic ginger carrots. Serve with braised Chinese broccoli and deep-fried crispy noodles.

Garlic Ginger Carrots: Heat oil in pan, add garlic, ginger and carrots, cook, stirring, 1 minute. Add shallots, wine, water and chilli flakes, simmer, uncovered, about 20 minutes or until liquid is evaporated, stirring occasionally during cooking. Stir in oregano.

- Recipe best made just before serving.
- Freeze: Not suitable.
- Microwave: Not suitable.

BRAISED CHINESE BROCCOLI

40g butter
½ bunch (about 12 leaves) Chinese broccoli, shredded

Heat butter in pan, add broccoli, cook, stirring, until just wilted.

- Recipe best made just before serving.
- Freeze: Not suitable.
- Microwave: Suitable.

DEEP-FRIED CRISPY NOODLES

oil for deep-frying
40g vermicelli noodles

Heat oil in pan, add noodles, cook until noodles are puffed and white; drain on absorbent paper.

- Recipe best made just before serving.
- Freeze: Not suitable.
- Microwave: Not suitable.

LEFT: Steak with Garlic Ginger Carrots, Braised Chinese Broccoli and Deep-Fried Crispy Noodles.

China and cutlery from Studio-Haus; glass from Villeroy & Boch.

Sausage, Onion and Olive Salad with Pasta

SAUSAGE, ONION AND OLIVE SALAD WITH PASTA

4 thick beef sausages
200g pasta spirals
2 medium (about 260g) tomatoes
⅔ cup black olives
1 red Spanish onion, sliced
1 small green pepper, sliced

DRESSING
1 tablespoon tarragon vinegar
¼ cup olive oil
1 clove garlic, crushed
¼ teaspoon sugar
5 green shallots, chopped

Grill or pan-fry sausages until cooked through, drain on absorbent paper; cool. Cut sausages into 2cm slices.

Add pasta to pan of boiling water, boil, uncovered, until pasta is just tender; drain.

Cut tomatoes into wedges. Combine sausages, pasta and tomatoes with remaining ingredients in bowl, drizzle salad with dressing.

Dressing: Combine all ingredients in jar; shake well.

- Recipe can be prepared 3 hours ahead. Add dressing just before serving.
- Storage: Salad and dressing separately, covered, in refrigerator.
- Freeze: Not suitable.
- Microwave: Pasta suitable.

ABOVE: Sausage, Onion and Olive Salad with Pasta.

Minced Beef and Caper Burgers

Fresh Beetroot with Herbs

Broccoli Puree

MINCED BEEF AND CAPER BURGERS

500g minced beef
4 green shallots, chopped
1½ tablespoons drained capers, chopped
1 egg, lightly beaten
1 clove garlic, crushed
1 small beef stock cube
1 tablespoon oil

Combine mince, shallots, capers, egg, garlic and crumbled stock cube in bowl; mix well. Shape into 4 burgers.

Heat oil in pan, add burgers, cook until browned on both sides and cooked through. Serve with fresh beetroot with herbs and broccoli puree.

- Burgers can be prepared 3 hours ahead.
- Storage: Covered, in refrigerator.
- Freeze: Uncooked burgers suitable.
- Microwave: Not suitable.

FRESH BEETROOT WITH HERBS

3 (about 300g) fresh beetroot
30g butter
3 teaspoons chopped fresh chives
3 teaspoons chopped fresh parsley

Boil, steam or microwave beetroot until tender, drain; cool, peel. Cut beetroot into ½cm slices, cut slices into strips. Heat butter in pan, add beetroot and herbs, stir over heat until heated through.

- Recipe can be prepared a day ahead.
- Storage: Covered, in refrigerator.
- Freeze: Not suitable.
- Microwave: Suitable.

BROCCOLI PUREE

400g broccoli
2 cups chicken stock
1 clove garlic, crushed
½ teaspoon chicken stock powder
¼ cup cream

Cut 8 small flowerettes from broccoli. Boil, steam or microwave flowerettes until just tender; drain, keep warm. Chop remaining broccoli with stems, add to pan with stock and garlic, simmer, covered, stirring occasionally, until broccoli is tender. Drain broccoli, reserving 1½ tablespoons liquid.

Blend or process chopped broccoli with reserved liquid and stock powder until smooth. Return mixture to pan, add cream, stir over heat until heated through. Serve puree topped with flowerettes.

- Recipe best made just before serving.
- Freeze: Not suitable.
- Microwave: Suitable.

RIGHT: Minced Beef and Caper Burgers, Fresh Beetroot with Herbs and Broccoli Puree.

China from Mikasa.

Satay Beef Spare Ribs

Sesame Salad

SATAY BEEF SPARE RIBS

180ml can coconut milk
1 teaspoon ground ginger
1 teaspoon garam masala
1 teaspoon ground coriander
1 teaspoon turmeric
¼ cup lemon juice
2 tablespoons crunchy peanut butter
3 cloves garlic, crushed
1 small onion, finely chopped
6 beef spare ribs

Combine all ingredients in large bowl; mix well. Cover, refrigerate mixture several hours or overnight.

Drain ribs, discard marinade. Grill or barbecue ribs until tender. Serve with sesame salad.

■ Recipe can be prepared a day ahead.
■ Storage: Covered, in refrigerator.
■ Freeze: Marinated ribs suitable.
■ Microwave: Not suitable.

SESAME SALAD

¼ oak leaf lettuce
1 stick celery, sliced
1 small green cucumber, sliced
6 cherry tomatoes, halved
¼ red pepper, thinly sliced

SESAME DRESSING
1 tablespoon sesame seeds, toasted
2 tablespoons lemon juice
1 tablespoon olive oil
½ teaspoon sugar

Combine torn lettuce leaves, remaining ingredients and dressing in large bowl; mix well.
Sesame Dressing: Combine all ingredients in jar; shake well.

■ Recipe best made just before serving.
■ Freeze: Not suitable.

LEFT: Satay Beef Spare Ribs with Sesame Salad.

China and cutlery from Limoges; glass from Villeroy & Boch.

Beef Fillets with Spiced Honey Sauce

Mushroom and Pepper Timbales

BEEF FILLETS WITH SPICED HONEY SAUCE

1 medium (about 120g) carrot
4 green shallots
100g green beans
1 tablespoon oil
4 small beef eye-fillet steaks

SPICED HONEY SAUCE
15g butter
1/2 teaspoon grated fresh ginger
1 teaspoon honey
2 teaspoons light soy sauce
2 teaspoons Worcestershire sauce
1 tablespoon water

Cut carrot into thin 10cm strips. Cut shallots and beans into 10cm lengths. Boil, steam or microwave vegetables until just tender, drain.

Heat oil in pan, add steaks, cook until tender and done as desired. Serve steaks with vegetables, drizzled with spiced honey sauce. Serve with mushroom and pepper timbales.

Spiced Honey Sauce: Heat butter in pan, add ginger, cook, stirring, about 1 minute or until aromatic. Add honey, sauces and water, stir over heat until boiling.

■ Beef fillets best cooked just before serving. Spiced honey sauce can be prepared 3 hours ahead.
■ Storage: Sauce, covered, in refrigerator.
■ Freeze: Not suitable.
■ Microwave: Vegetables suitable.

MUSHROOM AND PEPPER TIMBALES

2 tablespoons white rice
15g butter
50g mushrooms, chopped
1/2 small red pepper, finely chopped
1 tablespoon chopped fresh chives
2 teaspoons chopped fresh coriander

Add rice to pan of boiling water, boil, uncovered, until tender; drain.

Heat butter in pan, add mushrooms and pepper, cook, stirring, until mushrooms are soft. Add rice and herbs, stir until rice is heated through. Press mixture into 2 greased moulds (1/2 cup capacity), stand 5 minutes before turning out.

■ Recipe can be prepared a day ahead.
■ Storage: Covered, in refrigerator.
■ Freeze: Not suitable.
■ Microwave: Rice suitable.

ABOVE: Beef Fillets with Spiced Honey Sauce and Mushroom and Pepper Timbales.

Braised Meatballs with Cabbage

Potato Bread

BRAISED MEATBALLS WITH CABBAGE

1 thick slice bread
2 tablespoons milk
180g minced beef
1 egg yolk
2 tablespoons chopped fresh parsley
½ small onion, finely chopped
½ bacon rasher, finely chopped
1½ tablespoons grated parmesan cheese
⅓ cup packaged breadcrumbs
2 tablespoons packaged breadcrumbs, extra
2 tablespoons oil
¼ medium cabbage, shredded
425g can tomatoes, drained, chopped

Remove crusts from bread, place bread in bowl, add milk, stand 5 minutes. Stir in mince, yolk, parsley, onion, bacon, cheese and breadcrumbs; mix well. Roll level tablespoons of mixture into balls, toss meatballs in extra breadcrumbs. Heat half the oil in pan, add meatballs, cook until browned and cooked through; drain on absorbent paper.

Heat remaining oil in pan, add cabbage, cook, stirring, until tender. Stir in tomatoes, then meatballs, cook, covered, until hot. Serve with potato bread.

■ Recipe can be made a day ahead.
■ Storage: Covered, in refrigerator.
■ Freeze: Uncooked meatballs suitable.
■ Microwave: Not suitable.

POTATO BREAD

1 medium (about 150g) potato
2 teaspoons (7g) dried yeast
¼ cup warm water
2 cups plain flour
pinch salt
¼ cup warm milk

Grease 8cm x 26cm bar cake pan. Boil, steam or microwave potato until tender, drain; mash, cool.

Cream yeast with a little of the water in small bowl. Sift flour and salt into large bowl, rub in potato. Stir in yeast mixture, remaining water and milk; mix to a firm dough. Turn dough onto lightly floured surface, knead about 5 minutes or until dough is smooth and elastic. Return dough to large greased bowl, cover, stand in warm place about 2 hours or until dough is doubled in size.

Turn dough onto lightly floured surface, knead until smooth, shape to fit prepared pan. Cover with damp cloth, leave to rise 1 hour or until dough is doubled in size. Bake in moderate oven about 45 minutes or until bread is brown and sounds hollow when tapped.

■ Bread best made on day of serving.
■ Freeze: Suitable.
■ Microwave: Potato suitable.

LEFT: Braised Meatballs with Cabbage and Potato Bread.

China and fork from The Country Trader.

LAMB

Choice little centres of lamb cutlets with piquant peppercorn sauce and unusual vegetable terrines are among the treats to remember here. There's also the light taste of herbs and honey in a rolled loin, a tasty tomato sesame crust on racks of lamb, and glazed lamb cutlets with tangy fruit relish. Smart, too, in rustic style, is a hearty casserole using lamb shanks; these look almost more than a meal but are good eating and good value!

Lamb and Sun-Dried Tomato Parcels

Stir-Fried Green Vegetables

LAMB AND SUN-DRIED TOMATO PARCELS

1 tablespoon olive oil
1 clove garlic, crushed
300g lamb fillets, thinly sliced
2 tablespoons drained chopped
   sun-dried tomatoes
100g feta cheese, chopped
2 tablespoons chopped fresh basil
2 tablespoons sour cream
4 sheets fillo pastry
60g butter, melted
½ teaspoon poppy seeds

Heat oil in pan, add garlic and lamb, cook, stirring, until lamb is lightly browned and just tender. Transfer lamb to bowl, stir in tomatoes, cheese and basil; cool.

Stir cream into lamb mixture. Layer 2 pastry sheets together, brush each with butter, fold in half to form a square. Place half lamb mixture in centre of 1 square, fold pastry around filling to form a parcel. Repeat with remaining pastry, butter and filling. Place parcels seam side down on oven tray; brush with remaining butter, sprinkle with seeds.

Bake, uncovered, in hot oven about 10 minutes or until parcels are browned and heated through. Serve parcels with stir-fried green vegetables.

- Parcels can be prepared a day ahead.
- Storage: Covered, in refrigerator.
- Freeze: Not suitable.
- Microwave: Not suitable.

STIR-FRIED GREEN VEGETABLES

½ bunch (6 spears) fresh asparagus
1 tablespoon olive oil
100g snow peas
100g green beans
1 teaspoon seasoned pepper

Cut asparagus spears in half. Heat oil in pan or wok, add vegetables, stir-fry until just tender; stir in pepper.

- Recipe best made just before serving.
- Freeze: Not suitable.
- Microwave: Suitable.

RIGHT: Lamb and Sun-Dried Tomato Parcels with Stir-Fried Green Vegetables.

Taitu china from David Jones, Sydney; fork from Bibelot; salt and pepper set from Georg Jensen; tiles from Pazotti.

Lamb with Peppercorn Sauce

Vegetable Terrines

Minted New Potatoes

LAMB WITH PEPPERCORN SAUCE

2 racks of lamb (4 cutlets each)
20g butter
1 tablespoon brandy
⅓ cup cream
2 teaspoons drained green peppercorns

Remove meat from lamb racks, discard bones and fat. Heat butter in pan, add lamb, cook until well browned all over, reserve unwashed pan for sauce.

Transfer lamb to baking dish. Bake, uncovered, in moderately slow oven about 20 minutes or until tender. Remove lamb from dish, reserve juices.

Add brandy to reserved pan, ignite brandy, allow flames to subside. Add reserved juices, cream and peppercorns, cook, stirring, until mixture boils and thickens slightly. Serve sauce with lamb. Serve lamb with vegetable terrines and minted new potatoes.

- Recipe best made just before serving.
- Freeze: Not suitable.
- Microwave: Not suitable.

VEGETABLE TERRINES

1 medium nashi
½ medium (about 150g) eggplant
1 medium (about 150g) tomato
1 tablespoon oil
½ teaspoon celery salt
1 teaspoon chopped fresh coriander

Lightly oil 2 ovenproof dishes (½ cup capacity). Cut nashi, eggplant and tomato into 5mm slices. Heat oil in pan, cook nashi and eggplant until lightly browned; drain on absorbent paper. Layer nashi, eggplant, tomato, salt and coriander in prepared dishes (you should have about 3 layers).

Place piece of plastic wrap over vegetables, press down firmly, wrap plastic firmly around top of dishes. Bake in moderately slow oven about 20 minutes or until terrines are heated through. Unmould terrines onto plates, drain well. Transfer terrines to serving plates.

- Recipe can be prepared 4 hours ahead.
- Storage: Covered, in refrigerator.
- Freeze: Not suitable.
- Microwave: Not suitable.

MINTED NEW POTATOES

200g baby potatoes
30g butter
1 teaspoon chopped fresh mint

Boil, steam or microwave potatoes until just tender; drain. Toss potatoes in combined butter and mint.

- Recipe best made just before serving.
- Freeze: Not suitable.
- Microwave: Suitable.

ABOVE: Lamb with Peppercorn Sauce, Vegetable Terrines and Minted New Potatoes.

Lamb Shank Casserole

Creamy Leek Potatoes

LAMB SHANK CASSEROLE

2 (about 500g) lamb shanks
plain flour
1 tablespoon oil
1 onion, chopped
1 clove garlic, crushed
1 stick celery, chopped
1 large (about 150g) parsnip, chopped
¼ cup dry red wine
1 cup tomato puree
1 cup beef stock
1 bay leaf
1 teaspoon seasoned pepper
1 carrot, chopped
1 tablespoon chopped fresh parsley

Toss shanks in flour, shake away excess flour. Heat oil in pan, add shanks, cook until browned all over; remove from pan.

Add onion, garlic, celery and parsnip to same pan, cook, stirring, until onion is soft. Add wine, simmer, stirring, until reduced by half. Return shanks to pan, stir in puree, stock, bay leaf and pepper, simmer, covered, about 1 hour or until shanks are tender. Add carrot to pan, simmer, uncovered, about 10 minutes or until carrot is tender, discard bay leaf; stir in parsley. Serve with creamy leek potatoes.

■ Recipe can be made a day ahead.
■ Storage: Covered, in refrigerator.
■ Freeze: Suitable.
■ Microwave: Not suitable.

ABOVE: Lamb Shank Casserole with Creamy Leek Potatoes.

China from Villeroy & Boch.

CREAMY LEEK POTATOES

2 large (about 500g) potatoes, chopped
30g butter
1 clove garlic, crushed
½ small leek, finely chopped
½ teaspoon seasoned pepper

Boil, steam or microwave potatoes until tender; drain, mash well. Return potato to hot pan, stir over heat about 1 minute or until dry. Heat butter in pan, add garlic, leek and pepper, cook, stirring, until leek is soft. Add potato, stir until combined and heated through.

■ Recipe best made just before serving.
■ Freeze: Not suitable.
■ Microwave: Potatoes suitable.

FRUITY LAMB WITH COUSCOUS

4 (about 400g) lamb fillets
2 tablespoons olive oil
1 onion, finely chopped
3 cloves garlic, crushed
2 tablespoons finely chopped
   fresh ginger
1 teaspoon ground cumin
1 teaspoon paprika
¼ teaspoon chilli powder
1 teaspoon ground coriander
¼ cup blanched almonds, chopped
⅓ cup chopped raisins
2 tablespoons light soy sauce
1 tablespoon dry red wine

COUSCOUS
½ cup water
¾ cup couscous
20g butter
1 tablespoon chopped fresh
   coriander

Cut lamb into thin strips. Heat oil in pan, add onion, garlic and ginger, cook, stirring, until onion is soft. Add lamb and spices, stir over heat until lamb is browned and tender. Stir in nuts, raisins, sauce and wine, stir until heated through. Serve lamb with couscous. Serve with snow pea and shallot salad.

Couscous: Bring water to boil in pan, remove from heat, stir in couscous; stand about 3 minutes without stirring or until water is absorbed.

   Return pan to heat, stir in butter and coriander, stir until heated through.

◼ Recipe best made just before serving.
◼ Freeze: Not suitable.
◼ Microwave: Not suitable.

SNOW PEA AND SHALLOT SALAD

80g snow peas
80g sugar snap peas
1 small green cucumber
1 green shallot

SHALLOT DRESSING
2 tablespoons lime juice
1 tablespoon honey
2 green shallots, chopped
¼ cup oil

Boil, steam or microwave both peas until just tender, rinse under cold water; drain. Cut cucumber and shallot into 4cm lengths. Combine all ingredients in bowl, pour over dressing; mix well.

Shallot Dressing: Combine all ingredients in jar; shake well.

◼ Recipe best made just before serving.
◼ Freeze: Not suitable.
◼ Microwave: Peas suitable.

LEFT: Fruity Lamb with Couscous and Snow Pea and Shallot Salad.

Basket, serviette and ceramic bowls from Accoutrement; glass salad bowl and wine glass from Home & Garden; cutlery and serving spoon from Corso de Fiori.

Minty Lamb and Broccoli Salad

Garlic Parmesan Rolls

MINTY LAMB AND BROCCOLI SALAD

300g lamb fillets
1 tablespoon light soy sauce
1 tablespoon oil
400g broccoli, chopped
100g snow peas
1 medium zucchini
½ x 250g punnet cherry tomatoes
½ cup bean sprouts

DRESSING
1 tablespoon balsamic vinegar
1 tablespoon lemon juice
2 tablespoons olive oil
1 teaspoon sugar
1 small clove garlic, crushed
1 tablespoon chopped fresh mint

Combine lamb and sauce in bowl, cover, refrigerate 3 hours or overnight.

Heat oil in pan, add lamb, cook until browned and tender; cool.

Boil, steam or microwave broccoli and snow peas until tender, rinse under cold water; drain well. Using a vegetable peeler, peel zucchini into ribbons.

Combine sliced lamb, broccoli, snow peas, zucchini, tomatoes and sprouts in bowl. Pour dressing over salad; mix well. Serve with garlic parmesan rolls.

Dressing: Combine all ingredients in jar; shake well.

- Recipe best made just before serving.
- Freeze: Not suitable.
- Microwave: Broccoli and snow peas suitable.

ABOVE: Minty Lamb and Broccoli Salad with Garlic Parmesan Rolls.

Tray, bowl, tumblers and wine cooler from Casa Shopping; glass salad bowl from Villeroy & Boch; salad servers from The Design Shop; serviette from Accoutrement.

GARLIC PARMESAN ROLLS

50g butter, softened
¼ cup grated parmesan cheese
1 clove garlic, crushed
2 bread rolls

Combine butter, cheese and garlic in bowl; mix well. Slice rolls at 2cm intervals without cutting through base. Spread slices with butter, wrap each roll in foil. Bake in moderate oven about 15 minutes or until heated through.

- Recipe can be prepared 4 hours ahead.
- Storage: Covered, in refrigerator.
- Freeze: Uncooked rolls suitable.
- Microwave: Not suitable.

Bean and Lamb Stew

Avocado and Mushroom Salad

BEAN AND LAMB STEW

2 large (about 500g) lamb leg chops
1 tablespoon oil
2 teaspoons oil, extra
1 small onion, chopped
3 teaspoons plain flour
⅓ cup dry white wine
½ cup cream
2 tablespoons water
½ red pepper, thinly sliced
310g can cannellini beans, rinsed,
  drained

Remove meat from chops, cut into 3cm pieces. Heat oil in pan, add lamb, cook, stirring, until lightly browned all over, remove from pan.

Add extra oil and onion to same pan, cook, stirring, until soft. Stir in flour, cook, stirring, until mixture is dry and grainy. Remove pan from heat, gradually stir in combined wine, cream and water. Stir over heat until mixture boils and thickens, stir in lamb.

Pour mixture into ovenproof dish (4 cup capacity). Bake, covered, in moderate oven 30 minutes. Add pepper and beans, cook, covered, further 10 minutes or until lamb is tender. Serve with avocado and mushroom salad.

■ Recipe can be made 2 days ahead.
■ Storage: Covered, in refrigerator.
■ Freeze: Suitable.
■ Microwave: Suitable.

AVOCADO AND MUSHROOM SALAD

½ butter lettuce
½ small green cucumber, sliced
½ small avocado, chopped
1 green shallot, chopped
60g baby mushrooms, sliced

DRESSING
2 tablespoons cider vinegar
2 tablespoons olive oil
¼ teaspoon sugar
1 teaspoon chopped fresh rosemary
1 clove garlic, crushed

Combine torn lettuce leaves, cucumber, avocado, shallots and mushrooms in bowl, add dressing, toss lightly.
Dressing: Combine all ingredients in jar; shake well.

■ Recipe best made just before serving.
■ Freeze: Not suitable.

LEFT: Bean and Lamb Stew with Avocado and Mushroom Salad.

China, glasses and fork from Appley Hoare Antiques.

Lamb with Honey and Herb Seasoning

Rosemary Potatoes

Tomatoes and Broad Beans

LAMB WITH HONEY AND HERB SEASONING

¼ cup olive oil
2 teaspoons grated fresh ginger
1 clove garlic, crushed
1 tablespoon honey
1 tablespoon light soy sauce
¼ cup chopped fresh chives
½ cup chopped fresh basil
1 tablespoon chopped fresh tarragon
1 tablespoon chopped fresh oregano
1 small (about 900g) loin of lamb, boned

Blend or process oil, ginger, garlic, honey, soy sauce and herbs until smooth. Spread half the herb mixture over inside surface of lamb, roll up, tie at 3cm intervals. Reserve remaining herb mixture.

Place lamb on wire rack in baking dish, brush with some of remaining herb mixture. Bake in moderately hot oven about 45 minutes or until lamb is tender; cover with foil during cooking to prevent burning, if necessary. Stand 5 minutes before serving. Serve topped with remaining herb mixture. Serve with rosemary potatoes and tomatoes and broad beans.

■ Recipe can be prepared a day ahead.
■ Storage: Covered, in refrigerator.
■ Freeze: Not suitable.
■ Microwave: Not suitable.

ROSEMARY POTATOES

2 medium (about 300g) potatoes
20g butter, melted
½ teaspoon dried rosemary leaves
½ teaspoon garlic salt

Cut potatoes into thin slices. Place on greased oven tray in 4 flower shapes, overlapping slices in a single layer. Brush with butter, sprinkle with rosemary and garlic salt. Bake, uncovered, in moderately hot oven about 30 minutes or until browned and tender. Serve 2 flowers on top of each other.

■ Recipe best made just before serving.
■ Freeze: Not suitable.
■ Microwave: Not suitable.

TOMATOES AND BROAD BEANS

1 cup (180g) frozen broad beans
1 tablespoon oil
1 onion, sliced
425g can tomatoes

Boil, steam or microwave beans until tender, drain, cool slightly. Remove skins from beans.

Heat oil in pan, add onion, cook, stirring, until soft. Add undrained crushed tomatoes, bring to boil, simmer, uncovered, about 10 minutes or until most of the liquid is evaporated. Stir in beans, stir until heated through.

■ Recipe can be made a day ahead.
■ Storage: Covered, in refrigerator.
■ Freeze: Not suitable.
■ Microwave: Suitable.

RIGHT: Lamb with Honey and Herb Seasoning, Rosemary Potatoes and Tomatoes and Broad Beans.

China from Mikasa.

Racks of Lamb with Tomato Sesame Crust

Noodles with Carrots and Snow Peas

RACKS OF LAMB WITH TOMATO SESAME CRUST

2 racks of lamb (3 cutlets each)
¼ teaspoon sesame oil
1 tablespoon sesame seeds
3 teaspoons light soy sauce
3 teaspoons peanut butter
3 teaspoons sugar
1 baby onion, grated
3 teaspoons tomato paste

Trim fat from lamb. Combine remaining ingredients in bowl. Spread sesame mixture over lamb racks, place on wire rack in baking dish. Bake, uncovered, in moderately hot oven 20 minutes; cover with greased foil, bake further 10 minutes or until lamb is tender. Serve lamb with noodles with carrots and snow peas.

- Recipe can be prepared 4 hours ahead.
- Storage: Covered, in refrigerator.
- Freeze: Not suitable.
- Microwave: Not suitable.

NOODLES WITH CARROTS AND SNOW PEAS

100g fresh egg noodles
2 small carrots
2 teaspoons oil
1 clove garlic, crushed
1 teaspoon grated fresh ginger
100g snow peas, chopped
1 teaspoon light soy sauce
1 tablespoon hoi sin sauce

Add noodles to pan of boiling water, boil, uncovered, until tender; drain.

Cut carrots into thin 5cm strips. Heat oil in pan or wok, add garlic and ginger, stir-fry about 1 minute or until aromatic. Add carrots, snow peas and sauces, stir-fry until vegetables are just tender. Add noodles, stir-fry until heated through.

- Recipe best made just before serving.
- Freeze: Not suitable.
- Microwave: Noodles suitable.

ABOVE: Racks of Lamb with Tomato Sesame Crust and Noodles with Carrots and Snow Peas.

Glazed Lamb Cutlets with Tropical Relish

Jasmine Rice

GLAZED LAMB CUTLETS WITH TROPICAL RELISH

1 tablespoon chopped fresh
   lemon grass
1 teaspoon fish sauce
¼ cup light soy sauce
1 teaspoon sweet chilli sauce
1 tablespoon sugar
1 clove garlic, crushed
1 tablespoon grated fresh ginger
6 lamb cutlets

TROPICAL RELISH
¼ cup raspberry vinegar
1½ tablespoons red wine vinegar
½ cup dry white wine
¼ cup chopped dried pineapple
¼ cup chopped dried pear
2 tablespoons chopped dried mango
½ small apple, chopped
½ orange, chopped
¼ red pepper, thinly sliced
1½ tablespoons honey
3 black peppercorns
1 bay leaf
1 tablespoon chopped fresh
   coriander

Combine lemon grass, sauces, sugar, garlic and ginger in bowl. Add cutlets, cover, refrigerate 3 hours or overnight.

Drain cutlets from marinade, reserve marinade. Place cutlets on wire rack in baking dish, bake, uncovered, in moderately hot oven about 25 minutes or until tender, brushing occasionally with reserved marinade. Serve with tropical relish and jasmine rice.

Tropical Relish: Combine vinegars and wine in pan, simmer, uncovered, 3 minutes. Add fruit, pepper, honey, peppercorns and bay leaf. Simmer, uncovered, about 10 minutes or until mixture thickens. Discard bay leaf, stir in coriander; cool.

- Tropical relish can be made 3 days ahead.
- Storage: Covered, in refrigerator.
- Freeze: Not suitable.
- Microwave: Relish suitable.

JASMINE RICE

¾ cup jasmine rice
2 cups water

Place rice in strainer, rinse under cold water until water is clear. Combine the 2 cups water and rice in heavy-based pan, bring to boil, stirring, reduce heat, simmer gently, covered with tight-fitting lid, 10 minutes. Remove from heat, stand, covered, 10 minutes. It is important not to remove lid during cooking and steaming. Fluff rice with fork.

- Recipe best made just before serving.
- Freeze: Not suitable.
- Microwave: Not suitable.

ABOVE: Glazed Lamb Cutlets with Tropical Relish and Jasmine Rice.

China from Limoges; cutlery from Bibelot; tiles from Pazotti.

LAMB KEBABS WITH RATATOUILLE

2 large lamb leg steaks
2 cloves garlic, crushed
1/2 teaspoon cracked black
    peppercorns
8 baby mushrooms
1 teaspoon oil

RATATOUILLE
1/2 small eggplant
coarse cooking salt
1 tablespoon olive oil
1 small onion, sliced
1 clove garlic, crushed
1/2 small red pepper, sliced
1/2 small green pepper, sliced
1 medium (about 100g) zucchini,
    sliced
2 medium (about 260g) tomatoes,
    peeled, chopped
1/2 teaspoon chopped fresh oregano
1/2 teaspoon chopped fresh basil
2 tablespoons tomato puree

YOGURT SAUCE
1/2 cup plain yogurt
1 tablespoon chopped fresh oregano

Cut lamb into 3cm cubes, toss in combined garlic and peppercorns. Thread lamb and mushrooms onto 4 skewers; brush with oil. Grill kebabs until browned and tender. Serve with ratatouille and yogurt sauce. Serve with polenta wedges.
Ratatouille: Slice eggplant, sprinkle with salt, stand 20 minutes. Rinse eggplant under cold water, drain, pat dry with absorbent paper.

Heat oil in pan, add onion, garlic and peppers, cook, stirring, until onion is soft. Add eggplant, zucchini, tomatoes, herbs and puree, simmer, uncovered, about 20 minutes or until thick.
Yogurt Sauce: Combine all ingredients in bowl; mix well.

■ Recipe can be prepared a day ahead.
■ Storage: Covered, in refrigerator.
■ Freeze: Not suitable.
■ Microwave: Ratatouille suitable.

POLENTA WEDGES

10g butter
1/2 cup polenta
1 1/4 cups chicken stock
1 egg yolk
1/3 cup grated parmesan cheese
plain flour
oil for shallow-frying

Heat butter in pan, add polenta and stock. Stir until mixture boils, simmer, covered, about 12 minutes, stirring occasionally, until mixture is thickened.

Remove polenta from heat, stir in egg yolk and cheese. Spread mixture 1cm thick onto plate covered with plastic wrap. Refrigerate, uncovered, 1 hour.

Turn polenta onto board, cut into wedges, toss in flour, shake away excess flour. Shallow-fry polenta in hot oil in batches until lightly browned; drain on absorbent paper.

■ Recipe can be prepared a day ahead.
■ Storage: Covered, in refrigerator.
■ Freeze: Not suitable.
■ Microwave: Not suitable.

LEFT: Lamb Kebabs with Ratatouille and Polenta Wedges.

Plates and glasses from Accoutrement; tiles from Pazotti.

PORK & VEAL

Wasabi (or green horseradish) adds pungent flavour in our chilled butter served with

baked racks of veal; different and delicious! Pungent, too, are the green peppercorns

on the quick-cook pork steaks on this page. Other great tastes include veal

chops with eggplant seasoning and crispy potato rosti, veal meatballs with artichokes and

olives, and our quick ravioli with chilli salami sauce. And there's a terrific recipe

for spare rib fanciers!

Peppered Pork

Chinese Cabbage

Gingered Red Pepper

PEPPERED PORK

2 teaspoons drained green
**   peppercorns, crushed**
1 teaspoon sugar
2 pork butterfly steaks
1 tablespoon oil

Combine peppercorns and sugar in bowl, rub over both sides of steaks, cover, refrigerate 30 minutes. Heat oil in pan, add pork, cook until browned and tender. Serve pork with Chinese cabbage and gingered red pepper.

■ Recipe can be prepared a day ahead.
■ Storage: Covered, in refrigerator.
■ Freeze: Pork suitable.
■ Microwave: Not suitable.

CHINESE CABBAGE

30g butter
1 onion, sliced
2 cups shredded Chinese cabbage
2 teaspoons light soy sauce
2 tablespoons chopped fresh chives

Heat butter in pan, add onion, cook, stirring, until soft. Add cabbage, stir until just wilted, stir in sauce and chives.

■ Recipe best made just before serving.
■ Freeze: Not suitable.
■ Microwave: Suitable.

GINGERED RED PEPPER

20g butter
½ teaspoon grated fresh ginger
1 large red pepper, thinly sliced
2 teaspoons honey

Heat butter in pan, add ginger and pepper, cook, stirring, until pepper is just soft; stir in honey.

■ Recipe best made just before serving.
■ Freeze: Not suitable.
■ Microwave: Suitable.

RIGHT: Peppered Pork, Chinese Cabbage and Gingered Red Pepper.

China from Noritake.

Veal Chops with Eggplant Seasoning

Mini Potato Rosti

Peas with Spinach

Cut pocket in side of each chop, fill pockets with eggplant seasoning; secure with toothpicks. Heat oil in pan, add chops, cook until browned and tender. Serve with red pepper sauce. Serve with mini potato rosti and peas with spinach.

Eggplant Seasoning: Heat oil in pan, add shallot, garlic and eggplant, cook, stirring, until vegetables are soft; remove from heat, stir in breadcrumbs and basil.

Red Pepper Sauce: Quarter pepper, remove seeds and membrane. Grill skin side up until skin blisters and blackens. Remove skin from pepper; chop pepper. Blend pepper, oil and vinegar until smooth. Transfer mixture to pan, stir over heat until warm.

- Recipe can be prepared a day ahead.
- Storage: Covered, in refrigerator.
- Freeze: Seasoned chops suitable.
- Microwave: Eggplant seasoning suitable.

MINI POTATO ROSTI

2 large (about 400g) potatoes
⅓ cup oil

Lightly grease 4 egg rings. Coarsely grate potatoes. Heat oil in pan, add egg rings, press potato mixture evenly into egg rings. Cook gently about 5 minutes each side or until rosti are well browned and potato is tender.

- Recipe best made just before serving.
- Freeze: Not suitable.
- Microwave: Not suitable.

PEAS WITH SPINACH

30g butter
1 small onion, sliced
½ cup frozen peas, thawed
½ bunch (about 20 leaves) English spinach
1 small chicken stock cube
½ teaspoon cracked black peppercorns

Heat butter in pan or wok, add onion, cook, stirring, until soft. Stir in peas, cook 1 minute, stir in spinach, crumbled stock cube and pepper, cook, stirring, until vegetables are just tender.

- Recipe best made just before serving.
- Freeze: Not suitable.
- Microwave: Suitable.

VEAL CHOPS WITH EGGPLANT SEASONING

2 large (about 450g) veal chops
2 teaspoons olive oil

EGGPLANT SEASONING
2 teaspoons olive oil
1 green shallot, chopped
1 clove garlic, crushed
1 small (about 100g) eggplant, finely chopped
2 tablespoons stale breadcrumbs
1 tablespoon chopped fresh basil

RED PEPPER SAUCE
1 red pepper
1 tablespoon olive oil
1 teaspoon balsamic vinegar

LEFT: Veal Chops with Eggplant Seasoning, Mini Potato Rosti and Peas with Spinach.

Veal and Snow Pea Stir-Fry

VEAL AND SNOW PEA STIR-FRY

2 veal schnitzels, thinly sliced
2 teaspoons seeded mustard
1 medium (about 100g) zucchini
100g rice vermicelli
1 tablespoon oil
1 onion, quartered
1 clove garlic, crushed
80g snow peas
80g baby mushrooms, sliced
½ yellow pepper, thinly sliced
½ red pepper, thinly sliced
½ cup bean sprouts

1 tablespoon chopped fresh tarragon
½ cup sour cream
⅓ cup beef stock

Combine veal and mustard in bowl, cover, refrigerate 30 minutes.

Cut zucchini into 4cm strips. Place vermicelli in bowl, cover with hot water, cover, stand 5 minutes; drain.

Meanwhile, heat half the oil in pan or wok, add veal, stir-fry 1 minute, drain on absorbent paper. Heat remaining oil in pan, add onion and garlic, stir-fry 2 minutes. Add zucchini, peas, mushrooms, peppers and sprouts, stir-fry 2 minutes. Return veal to pan, add tarragon, cream and stock, stir-fry until mixture boils and is well combined. Serve with vermicelli.

■ Recipe best made just before serving.
■ Freeze: Not suitable.
■ Microwave: Not suitable.

BELOW: Veal and Snow Pea Stir-Fry.

Wok from Corso de Fiori; bowls from The Design Store; pine tray from Accoutrement; cloth and place mat from Remo; salt dish and stir-fry spoon from Butler & Co.

ORIENTAL PORK SPARE RIBS

1 tablespoon hoi sin sauce
1 tablespoon light soy sauce
2 teaspoons grated fresh ginger
1 clove garlic, crushed
1 tablespoon dry sherry
½ teaspoon sugar
1 tablespoon honey
4 (about 700g) pork spare ribs
1 tablespoon oil

Combine sauces, ginger, garlic, sherry, sugar and honey in bowl, add ribs, cover, refrigerate 3 hours or overnight.

Drain ribs from marinade, reserve marinade. Heat oil in pan, cook ribs until browned and cooked through. Add reserved marinade to pan, simmer, stirring, until sauce thickens and ribs are coated. Serve with shredded vegetables with soy sauce.

- Recipe can be prepared a day ahead.
- Storage: Covered, in refrigerator.
- Freeze: Marinated ribs suitable.
- Microwave: Not suitable.

SHREDDED VEGETABLES WITH SOY SAUCE

1 small onion
1 medium carrot
1 zucchini
1 tablespoon oil
1 small red pepper, sliced
60g snow peas
12 leaves bok choy, shredded
12 leaves choy sum, shredded
⅓ cup bean sprouts
1½ teaspoons cornflour
¼ cup water
1 tablespoon dry sherry
1 tablespoon light soy sauce
½ teaspoon chicken stock powder

Cut onion into wedges. Cut carrot and zucchini into thin sticks. Heat oil in pan or wok, add onion, carrot and zucchini, stir-fry 3 minutes. Add pepper and snow peas, stir-fry until vegetables are just tender. Add bok choy, choy sum and sprouts. Stir in blended cornflour and water, sherry, sauce and stock powder, stir over heat until sauce boils and thickens.

- Recipe best made just before serving.
- Freeze: Not suitable.
- Microwave: Suitable.

RIGHT: Oriental Pork Spare Ribs and Shredded Vegetables with Soy Sauce.
FAR RIGHT: Veal and Mushroom Ragout with Buttered Spinach and Honeyed Carrots.

Taitu china from David Jones, Sydney; cutlery from Christofle.

Oriental Pork Spare Ribs

Shredded Vegetables with Soy Sauce

Veal and Mushroom Ragout

Buttered Spinach

Honeyed Carrots

VEAL AND MUSHROOM RAGOUT

1 tablespoon oil
400g diced veal
30g butter
1 onion, sliced
200g mushrooms, sliced
1½ tablespoons plain flour
¼ cup dry white wine
½ cup water
½ cup sour cream
½ teaspoon dried thyme leaves
2 tablespoons sour cream, extra
½ avocado, chopped
2 x 125mm (60g) vol-au-vent cases

Heat oil in pan, add veal, cook, stirring, until browned; remove from pan. Heat butter in same pan, add onion, cook, stirring, until soft. Add mushrooms, cook, stirring, 2 minutes. Stir in flour, stir until mixture is dry and grainy. Remove pan from heat, gradually stir in wine, water, cream and thyme. Return veal to pan, stir over heat until mixture boils, simmer, partly covered, about 40 minutes or until tender. Stir in extra cream and avocado.

Place vol-au-vent cases on oven tray. Bake, uncovered, in moderate oven about 5 minutes or until heated through. Serve ragout in cases. Serve with buttered spinach and honeyed carrots.

- Can be prepared 2 days ahead. Fill cases just before serving.
- Storage: Covered, in refrigerator.
- Freeze: Not suitable.
- Microwave: Ragout suitable.

BUTTERED SPINACH

15g butter
1 small onion, finely chopped
1 bunch (40 leaves) English spinach
pinch nutmeg

Heat butter in pan, add onion, cook, stirring, until soft. Add spinach and nutmeg, cook, stirring, until spinach is just wilted.

- Recipe best made just before serving.
- Freeze: Not suitable.
- Microwave: Suitable.

HONEYED CARROTS

2 medium (about 240g) carrots, chopped
15g butter
2 teaspoons honey

Boil, steam or microwave carrots until tender, drain. Heat butter in pan, add carrots and honey, toss lightly.

- Recipe best made just before serving.
- Freeze: Not suitable.
- Microwave: Suitable.

Pork with Sour Cream Paprika Sauce

Herb Gnocchi

ABOVE: Pork with Sour Cream Paprika Sauce and Herb Gnocchi.

China from Villeroy & Boch; glasses from Accoutrement.

PORK WITH SOUR CREAM PAPRIKA SAUCE

1 (about 350g) pork fillet
plain flour
1 tablespoon oil

SOUR CREAM PAPRIKA SAUCE
20g butter
½ small onion, chopped
1 clove garlic, crushed
½ small green pepper, chopped
70g baby mushrooms, sliced
2 teaspoons plain flour
1 teaspoon paprika
½ teaspoon Worcestershire sauce
1 teaspoon lemon juice
2 teaspoons tomato paste
½ cup chicken stock
½ cup sour cream

Slice pork diagonally. Place slices between plastic wrap, flatten slightly with meat mallet. Dust pork with flour, shake away excess flour. Heat oil in pan, add pork, cook until browned and tender. Serve pork with sour cream paprika sauce. Serve with herb gnocchi.

Sour Cream Paprika Sauce: Heat butter in pan, add onion, garlic and pepper, cook, stirring, until onion is soft. Add mushrooms, cook, stirring, until mushrooms are tender. Add flour and paprika, stir until combined. Remove from heat, gradually stir in combined sauce, juice, paste and stock, simmer, uncovered, 5 minutes. Stir in sour cream, stir until heated through.

- Recipe best made just before serving.
- Freeze: Not suitable.
- Microwave: Sour cream paprika sauce suitable.

HERB GNOCCHI

250g old potatoes
60g ricotta cheese
2 teaspoons chopped fresh chives
2 teaspoons chopped fresh parsley
¼ cup plain flour
20g butter, melted

Boil, steam or microwave potatoes until tender, drain, press through sieve. Using hand, knead cheese and herbs into potato, then knead in sifted flour, gradually. Roll dough into log shape 2cm in diameter. Cut log into 1cm lengths, roll each length into a ball. Place each ball of dough into palm of hand, press dough with floured prongs of fork.

Add gnocchi to large pan of boiling water, simmer, uncovered, until gnocchi are tender; drain. Brush gnocchi with butter, serve sprinkled with grated parmesan cheese, if desired.

- Recipe can be made a day ahead.
- Storage: Covered, in refrigerator.
- Freeze: Suitable.
- Microwave: Potatoes suitable.

Veal Meatballs with Artichokes and Olives

Pasta with Peppers

VEAL MEATBALLS WITH ARTICHOKES AND OLIVES

250g minced veal
1 egg, lightly beaten
2 tablespoons chopped fresh parsley
2 tablespoons grated parmesan cheese
1/3 cup packaged breadcrumbs
2 tablespoons olive oil
1 small red Spanish onion, sliced
2 cloves garlic, crushed
1 cup (about 180g) pimiento-stuffed green olives, halved
2 tablespoons chopped fresh sage
425g can tomatoes
8 artichoke hearts, drained, halved

Combine mince, egg, parsley, cheese and breadcrumbs in bowl; mix well. Shape mixture into 6 balls. Heat half the oil in pan, add meatballs, cook until lightly browned; drain on absorbent paper.

Heat remaining oil in pan, add onion and garlic, cook, stirring, until onion is soft. Add olives, sage and undrained crushed tomatoes. Return meatballs to pan, simmer, covered, about 20 minutes or until meatballs are tender. Add artichokes to pan, stir until heated through. Serve with pasta with peppers.

- Recipe can be made a day ahead.
- Storage: Covered, in refrigerator.
- Freeze: Uncooked meatballs suitable.
- Microwave: Suitable.

PASTA WITH PEPPERS

1/2 cup penne pasta
2 teaspoons olive oil
1/2 small red Spanish onion, sliced
1/4 yellow pepper, sliced
1/4 green pepper, sliced
1/4 red pepper, sliced
1 teaspoon chopped fresh sage
1 teaspoon balsamic vinegar

Add pasta to pan of boiling water, boil, uncovered, until just tender; drain.

Meanwhile, heat oil in pan, add onion and peppers, cook, stirring, until onion is soft. Add pasta, sage and vinegar to pan, stir until heated through.

- Recipe best made just before serving.
- Freeze: Not suitable.
- Microwave: Pasta suitable.

LEFT: Veal Meatballs with Artichokes and Olives and Pasta with Peppers.

Racks of Veal with Wasabi Butter

Spicy Leeks and Mushrooms

Crispy Kumara Curls

RACKS OF VEAL WITH WASABI BUTTER

2 racks of veal (3 cutlets each)
2 teaspoons French mustard
2 teaspoons chopped fresh thyme
20g butter, melted

WASABI BUTTER
50g soft butter
½ teaspoon wasabi paste or powder
3 teaspoons chopped fresh chives
1 teaspoon chopped fresh thyme

Trim excess fat from veal. Combine mustard and thyme in bowl; mix well.

Place veal on wire rack in baking dish, spread with mustard mixture, drizzle with butter. Bake, uncovered, in moderate oven about 40 minutes or until veal is tender. Serve with wasabi butter. Serve with spicy leeks and mushrooms and crispy kumara curls.
Wasabi Butter: Combine all ingredients in bowl; mix well. Spoon butter mixture onto foil, roll up firmly into log shape; refrigerate until firm.

- Butter can be made 3 days ahead.
- Storage: Covered, in refrigerator.
- Freeze: Butter suitable.
- Microwave: Not suitable.

SPICY LEEKS AND MUSHROOMS

20g butter
2 small leeks, sliced
100g baby mushrooms, quartered
2 tablespoons dry white wine
pinch chilli flakes
¼ teaspoon onion salt

Heat butter in pan, add leeks and mushrooms, cook, stirring, until vegetables are just tender. Stir in wine, chilli flakes and salt, stir over heat 1 minute.

- Recipe best made just before serving.
- Freeze: Not suitable.
- Microwave: Suitable.

CRISPY KUMARA CURLS

300g (about 15cm long) kumara
oil for deep-frying

Peel thin strips from length of kumara using a vegetable peeler. You will need about 2 cups of strips (use remaining kumara for another purpose). Deep-fry kumara in hot oil in batches until curled and crisp; drain on absorbent paper.

- Recipe can be made 1 hour ahead.
- Storage: Covered, at room temperature.
- Freeze: Not suitable.
- Microwave: Not suitable.

LEFT: Racks of Veal with Wasabi Butter, Spicy Leeks and Mushrooms and Crispy Kumara Curls.

China from Wedgwood.

Marinated Pork with Beans and Tomatoes

Mushroom and Watercress Salad

MARINATED PORK WITH BEANS AND TOMATOES

⅓ cup haricot beans
2 pork butterfly steaks
1 tablespoon oil
1 small onion, chopped
410g can tomatoes
2 tablespoons dry red wine
2 teaspoons sugar

MARINADE
2 tablespoons red wine vinegar
2 cloves garlic, crushed
1 tablespoon olive oil
2 teaspoons chopped fresh basil

Place beans in bowl; cover with cold water, stand overnight. Add pork to marinade in bowl; cover, refrigerate several hours or overnight.

Drain beans, rinse well. Add beans to pan of boiling water, simmer, uncovered, about 1 hour or until tender; drain.

Drain pork, discard marinade. Heat oil in pan, add pork, cook until browned and tender. Remove pork from pan; keep warm. Add onion to same pan, cook, stirring, until onion is lightly browned. Stir in undrained crushed tomatoes, wine and sugar, simmer, uncovered, until sauce is thickened slightly. Add beans, stir until heated through. Serve pork with beans and tomatoes. Serve with mushroom and watercress salad.

Marinade: Combine all ingredients in bowl; mix well.

- Recipe can be prepared a day ahead.
- Storage: Covered, in refrigerator.
- Freeze: Marinated pork suitable.
- Microwave: Beans suitable.

MUSHROOM AND WATERCRESS SALAD

¼ cup olive oil
200g baby mushrooms, sliced
1 clove garlic, crushed
1 tablespoon balsamic vinegar
1 cup firmly packed watercress sprigs

Heat oil in pan, add mushrooms and garlic, cook, stirring, until mushrooms are lightly browned. Remove pan from heat, stir in vinegar; cool. Toss watercress through mushroom mixture.

- Recipe best made just before serving.
- Freeze: Not suitable.
- Microwave: Not suitable.

Ravioli with Chilli Salami Sauce

Artichoke and Avocado Salad

RAVIOLI WITH CHILLI SALAMI SAUCE

100g sliced mild salami
300g ravioli
2 large (about 500g) tomatoes, peeled, chopped
1 tablespoon chilli sauce
1½ tablespoons tomato paste
1 clove garlic, crushed
¼ cup parmesan cheese flakes

Cut salami into strips, add to dry pan, cook, stirring, until crisp; drain on absorbent paper. Add ravioli to large pan of boiling water, boil, uncovered, until just tender; drain on absorbent paper.

Blend or process tomatoes, sauce and paste until smooth. Transfer mixture to pan, add garlic, simmer, uncovered, about 5 minutes or until slightly thickened. Toss sauce through ravioli, sprinkle with salami and cheese. Serve with artichoke and avocado salad.

■ Sauce can be prepared a day ahead.
■ Storage: Covered, in refrigerator.
■ Freeze: Chilli salami sauce suitable.
■ Microwave: Suitable.

ARTICHOKE AND AVOCADO SALAD

½ x 160g punnet snow pea sprouts
8 artichoke hearts, drained
1 small avocado, sliced

BASIL DRESSING
¼ cup olive oil
1 tablespoon white vinegar
1 clove garlic, crushed
1 tablespoon chopped fresh basil

Arrange sprouts, artichokes and avocado on serving plates, drizzle salad with basil dressing.
Basil Dressing: Combine all ingredients in jar; shake well.

■ Recipe can be prepared 2 hours ahead.
■ Storage: Covered, in refrigerator.
■ Freeze: Not suitable.

ABOVE LEFT: Marinated Pork with Beans and Tomatoes and Mushroom and Watercress Salad.
LEFT: Ravioli with Chilli Salami Sauce and Artichoke and Avocado Salad.

Above left: China from Mikasa. Left: Pottery from Kenwick Galleries.

VEGETARIAN

Delicate creamed peas top a tasty tofu layer in quiches, and a second pastry recipe is as

easy as baking strips around cup shapes and filling with luscious ratatouille.

For colour, look no further than our cool red cabbage and beetroot salad. You can savour

chick pea and vegetable bake, pasta with vegetables carbonara and pizzas with

pesto and goats' cheese. Accompaniments include wholemeal mushroom muffins and

okra and tomato stew.

Zucchini Peanut Burgers

Okra and Tomato Stew

ZUCCHINI PEANUT BURGERS

2 (about 200g) zucchini, grated
½ cup roasted peanuts, chopped
2 eggs, lightly beaten
2 tablespoons chopped fresh parsley
½ cup cooked brown rice
½ cup stale breadcrumbs
plain flour
2 tablespoons oil

Squeeze excess moisture from zucchini. Combine zucchini, peanuts, eggs, parsley, rice and breadcrumbs in bowl. Shape into 6 burgers, toss in flour; heat oil in pan, cook burgers until browned. Serve with okra and tomato stew.

- Can be prepared 3 hours ahead.
- Storage: Covered, in refrigerator.
- Freeze: Not suitable.
- Microwave: Not suitable.

OKRA AND TOMATO STEW

1 tablespoon oil
1 onion, sliced
1 clove garlic, crushed
425g can tomatoes
12 (about 150g) okra
1 tablespoon chopped fresh parsley

Heat oil in pan, add onion and garlic, cook, stirring, until onion is soft. Add undrained crushed tomatoes, okra and parsley, simmer, covered, 20 minutes.

- Recipe can be made a day ahead.
- Storage: Covered, in refrigerator.
- Freeze: Not suitable.
- Microwave: Suitable.

RIGHT: Zucchini Peanut Burgers with Okra and Tomato Stew.

China from Mikasa.

Chick Pea and Vegetable Bake

Oregano Green Salad

Olive Bread

CHICK PEA AND VEGETABLE BAKE

1 tablespoon oil
1 small leek, sliced
1 stick celery, sliced
1 small carrot, chopped
1 zucchini, chopped
100g baby mushrooms, sliced
425g can tomatoes
¼ cup water
¼ cup dry white wine
2 tablespoons tomato paste
310g can chick peas, rinsed, drained
¼ teaspoon celery salt
1 tablespoon plain flour
2 tablespoons water, extra
2 tablespoons chopped fresh basil
1 large (about 200g) potato
20g butter, melted

Heat oil in pan, add leek, cook, stirring, until leek is soft. Add celery, carrot, zucchini and mushrooms, cook, stirring, 1 minute. Add undrained crushed tomatoes, water, wine, paste, chick peas and celery salt. Bring to boil, simmer, uncovered, about 15 minutes or until sauce thickens slightly. Stir in blended flour and extra water, stir until sauce boils and thickens; stir in basil.

Spoon mixture into 2 ovenproof dishes (2 cup capacity). Slice potato thinly, layer potato over mixture, brush with butter, sprinkle with a little extra celery salt. Bake, uncovered, in moderate oven about 1 hour or until potato is tender. Serve with oregano green salad and olive bread.

- Recipe can be prepared a day ahead. Potato best sliced just before cooking.
- Storage: Covered, in refrigerator.
- Freeze: Not suitable.
- Microwave: Not suitable.

OREGANO GREEN SALAD

250g broccoli, chopped
150g sugar snap peas
½ bunch (6 spears) fresh asparagus, chopped
4 lettuce leaves

DRESSING
¼ cup olive oil
2 tablespoons lemon juice
½ teaspoon sugar
1 clove garlic, crushed
1 tablespoon chopped fresh oregano

Add broccoli, peas and asparagus to pan of boiling water, drain; rinse under cold water, drain well. Combine vegetables in bowl, pour over dressing. Line bowl with lettuce, add salad.

Dressing: Combine all ingredients in jar; shake well.

- Recipe best made just before serving.
- Freeze: Not suitable.
- Microwave: Vegetables suitable.

Pasta with Vegetables Carbonara

Sweet and Sour Cabbage

OLIVE BREAD

80g soft butter
¼ cup black olives, finely chopped
1 clove garlic, crushed
½ teaspoon dried oregano leaves
1 small French bread stick

Combine butter, olives, garlic and oregano in bowl; mix well. Cut bread stick into slices, without cutting right through. Spread olive mixture between slices, wrap bread stick in foil. Bake bread in moderate oven about 10 minutes or until heated through.

◼ Recipe can be prepared several hours ahead.
◼ Storage: Covered, in refrigerator.
◼ Freeze: Unbaked bread suitable.
◼ Microwave: Not suitable.

LEFT: Chick Pea and Vegetable Bake with Oregano Green Salad and Olive Bread. ABOVE: Pasta with Vegetables Carbonara and Sweet and Sour Cabbage.

Left: China from Mikasa. Above: China from The Bay Tree.

PASTA WITH VEGETABLES CARBONARA

¾ cup cellantini pasta
1 tablespoon oil
1 small red Spanish onion, sliced
½ red pepper, chopped
80g snow peas, chopped
60g mushrooms, chopped
⅓ cup canned drained corn kernels
¼ cup grated parmesan cheese
¼ cup grated tasty cheese
½ cup sour cream
2 eggs, lightly beaten
½ teaspoon garlic salt
1 tablespoon chopped fresh chives
1 tablespoon chopped fresh basil

Add pasta to pan of boiling water, boil, uncovered, until just tender; drain.

Heat oil in pan, add onion, pepper, snow peas and mushrooms, cook, stirring, until onion is soft. Add pasta, corn, cheeses and sour cream, stir until well combined and heated through. Remove from heat, stir in eggs, salt and herbs, stir until combined and slightly thickened.

◼ Recipe best made just before serving.
◼ Freeze: Not suitable.
◼ Microwave: Suitable.

SWEET AND SOUR CABBAGE

1 tablespoon oil
1 small onion, sliced
¼ small red cabbage, shredded
⅓ cup cider vinegar
1 small apple, chopped

Heat oil in pan, add onion, cook, stirring, until soft. Add cabbage and vinegar, cook, covered, over very low heat, stirring occasionally, about 20 minutes. Stir in apple, cook, covered, about further 10 minutes or until apple and cabbage are soft.

◼ Recipe can be made a day ahead.
◼ Storage: Covered, in refrigerator.
◼ Freeze: Not suitable.
◼ Microwave: Suitable.

Tofu Quiches with Watercress Sauce

Carrot Ribbon Salad

TOFU QUICHES WITH WATERCRESS SAUCE

⅓ cup white plain flour
2 tablespoons wholemeal plain flour
50g butter
2 teaspoons sesame seeds, toasted
1 egg yolk
2 teaspoons water, approximately
2 tablespoons grated parmesan cheese
20g butter, extra
2 green shallots, chopped
2 cloves garlic, crushed
¼ red pepper, finely chopped
80g tofu, chopped
2 teaspoons chopped fresh basil
¼ cup peas
1 egg
¼ cup sour cream

WATERCRESS SAUCE
30g butter
1 clove garlic, crushed
4 green shallots, chopped
1 cup chopped watercress
¼ cup water
2 teaspoons chopped fresh basil
2 tablespoons cream

Grease 2 x 11cm flan tins. Sift flours into bowl, rub in butter, stir in seeds. Add egg yolk and enough water to mix to a firm dough. Knead on floured surface until smooth, cover, refrigerate 30 minutes.

Roll pastry on floured surface large enough to line prepared tins. Lift pastry into tins, ease into sides, trim edges. Place tins on oven tray, line pastry with paper, fill with dried beans or rice. Bake in moderately hot oven 8 minutes, remove paper and beans, bake about further 8 minutes or until browned; cool.

Sprinkle cheese into pastry cases. Heat extra butter in pan, add shallots, garlic and pepper, cook, stirring, until pepper is soft. Stir in tofu and basil. Spoon mixture into pastry cases. Boil, steam or microwave peas until soft; drain. Blend peas with egg and sour cream until smooth. Pour pea mixture carefully over tofu mixture. Bake in moderate oven about 30 minutes or until set. Serve warm with watercress sauce. Serve with carrot ribbon salad.

Watercress Sauce: Heat butter in pan, add garlic and shallots, cook, stirring, until shallots are soft. Stir in watercress, water and basil, simmer, covered, 5 minutes. Blend watercress mixture with cream. Return mixture to pan, stir until hot.

■ Quiches can be prepared a day ahead. Watercress sauce best made just before serving.
■ Storage: Covered, in refrigerator.
■ Freeze: Not suitable.
■ Microwave: Peas suitable.

CARROT RIBBON SALAD

1 medium carrot
¼ red pepper, sliced
2 tablespoons chopped roasted
    cashews

DRESSING
2 tablespoons oil
2 teaspoons white vinegar
2 teaspoons lemon juice
pinch sugar

Using a vegetable peeler, peel thin ribbons from length of carrot. Combine carrot, pepper and cashews in bowl; pour over dressing.
Dressing: Combine all ingredients in jar; shake well.

- ■ Recipe can be prepared 3 hours ahead.
- ■ Storage: Covered, in refrigerator.
- ■ Freeze: Not suitable.

Curried Vegetable Stew with Dhal

Pappadums

CURRIED VEGETABLE STEW WITH DHAL

1 medium (about 120g) carrot
2 small (about 130g) zucchini
¼ small red pepper
⅓ cup oil
1 onion, sliced
3 cloves garlic, crushed
2 teaspoons grated fresh ginger
¾ teaspoon turmeric
1 small fresh red chilli, finely chopped
1 teaspoon yellow mustard seeds
¾ teaspoon ground coriander
½ teaspoon cumin seeds
1 teaspoon cracked black
    peppercorns
¼ small cauliflower, chopped
1 large (about 250g) tomato, chopped
2 tablespoons chopped fresh parsley
80g green beans, chopped
⅓ cup water

DHAL
½ cup yellow split peas
2¾ cups water

Cut carrot and zucchini into 2cm sticks; cut pepper into 2cm squares. Heat oil in pan, add onion, garlic, ginger and spices, cook, stirring, until onion is soft. Add carrot, cauliflower, tomato and parsley, cook, stirring, 8 minutes. Stir in zucchini, pepper, beans, water and dhal, simmer, uncovered, stirring occasionally, about 15 minutes or until vegetables are tender. Serve curried vegetable stew with pappadums and rice, if desired.
Dhal: Cover peas with water in bowl, stand 2 hours. Drain peas, discard water. Combine peas and the 2¾ cups water in pan, simmer, uncovered, about 40 minutes or until peas are soft. Blend or process undrained peas until smooth.

- ■ Recipe can be made a day ahead.
- ■ Storage: Covered, in refrigerator.
- ■ Freeze: Not suitable.
- ■ Microwave: Suitable.

PAPPADUMS

4 large pappadums
oil for deep-frying

Add 1 pappadum to hot oil, deep-fry on both sides until puffed and golden; drain on absorbent paper. Repeat with remaining pappadums.

- ■ Recipe best made just before serving.
- ■ Freeze: Not suitable.
- ■ Microwave: Suitable without oil.

FAR LEFT: Tofu Quiches with Watercress Sauce and Carrot Ribbon Salad.
LEFT: Curried Vegetable Stew with Dhal and Pappadums.

Far left: China from The Bay Tree. Left: China from Villeroy & Boch; serviettes and place mat from Lillywhites.

111

Red Cabbage and Beetroot Salad

Mini Basil Loaves

RED CABBAGE AND BEETROOT SALAD

100g green beans, sliced
100g snow peas, sliced
¼ red cabbage, shredded
1 medium (about 160g) fresh beetroot, coarsely grated
2 tablespoons olive oil
2 tablespoons cider vinegar
½ cup pecans or walnuts
50g blue vein cheese, crumbled

CROUTES
1 torpedo wholemeal bread roll
40g butter, melted
1 tablespoon grated parmesan cheese

Boil, steam or microwave beans and snow peas separately until just tender, drain; rinse under cold water, drain well, pat dry with absorbent paper.

Combine beans, peas, cabbage, beetroot, oil, vinegar and nuts in bowl, toss lightly. Spoon salad onto serving plates, serve with cheese and croutes. Serve with mini basil loaves.

Croutes: Cut roll into thin slices, brush both sides with butter. Place in single layer on oven tray, sprinkle with cheese. Bake, uncovered, in moderate oven about 10 minutes or until crisp and browned.

■ Croutes can be made 3 days ahead.
■ Storage: Airtight container.
■ Freeze: Not suitable.
■ Microwave: Beans and snow peas suitable.

MINI BASIL LOAVES

1 cup self-raising flour
2 teaspoons butter
2 tablespoons chopped fresh basil
½ cup milk, approximately

Grease 2 x 6cm x 10cm individual loaf tins. Sift flour into bowl, rub in butter, stir in basil. Add enough milk to mix to a soft dough. Knead dough on floured surface until smooth. Divide dough into 4 portions, roll each portion into a ball. Place 2 balls in each prepared tin, brush with a little milk. Bake, uncovered, in moderately hot oven about 20 minutes or until loaves are browned and cooked through.

■ Recipe can be made a day ahead.
■ Storage: Airtight container.
■ Freeze: Suitable.
■ Microwave: Not suitable.

Minty Lentil Salad

Wholemeal Mushroom Muffins

MINTY LENTIL SALAD

¾ cup brown lentils
1 carrot, finely chopped
1 small onion, finely chopped
1 teaspoon vegetable stock paste
1 clove garlic, crushed
1 bay leaf
1 litre (4 cups) water
1 tablespoon chopped fresh mint
1 small butter lettuce
2 hard-boiled eggs, quartered
2 small tomatoes, quartered

VINAIGRETTE
½ cup olive oil
⅓ cup lemon juice
½ teaspoon paprika
1 teaspoon grated lemon rind

Rinse lentils under cold water; drain. Combine lentils, carrot, onion, paste, garlic, bay leaf and water in pan, simmer, uncovered, about 25 minutes or until lentils are tender.

Drain lentil mixture, discard bay leaf. Transfer mixture to bowl, stir in half the vinaigrette; cool. Cover lentil mixture, refrigerate until cold.

Stir in mint, serve over lettuce, top with eggs and tomatoes; drizzle with remaining vinaigrette. Serve with wholemeal mushroom muffins.

Vinaigrette: Combine all ingredients in jar; shake well.

■ Lentils can be prepared a day ahead.
■ Storage: Covered, in refrigerator.
■ Freeze: Not suitable.
■ Microwave: Suitable.

LEFT: Red Cabbage and Beetroot Salad with Mini Basil Loaves.
BELOW: Minty Lentil Salad with Wholemeal Mushroom Muffins.

Below: Pottery from Amy's Tableware.

WHOLEMEAL MUSHROOM MUFFINS

½ cup white self-raising flour
½ cup wholemeal self-raising flour
20g butter
2 tablespoons grated parmesan cheese
100g mushrooms, chopped
2 tablespoons chopped fresh chives
1 egg, lightly beaten
⅓ cup milk

Grease 4 holes (⅓ cup capacity) in muffin pan. Sift flours into bowl, rub in butter, stir in cheese, mushrooms, chives, egg and milk, mix until just combined. Spoon mixture into prepared pan. Bake in moderately hot oven about 25 minutes or until browned and cooked through.

■ Muffins are best made on day of serving.
■ Freeze: Suitable.
■ Microwave: Not suitable.

Pizzas with Pesto and Goats' Cheese

Watercress and Witlof Salad

PIZZAS WITH PESTO AND GOATS' CHEESE

2 teaspoons (7g) dried yeast
½ teaspoon sugar
1 teaspoon white plain flour
⅔ cup warm water
⅓ cup wholemeal plain flour
1⅓ cups white plain flour, extra
1 tablespoon olive oil
½ small red pepper, thinly sliced
100g mushrooms, sliced
4 artichoke hearts, drained, sliced
¼ cup drained sun-dried tomatoes, sliced
100g goats' cheese, sliced
1 tablespoon shredded fresh basil
1 tablespoon olive oil, extra

PESTO
2 cups firmly packed fresh basil leaves
¼ cup olive oil
2 cloves garlic, crushed
¼ cup grated parmesan cheese
2 tablespoons pine nuts, toasted

Combine yeast, sugar, the 1 teaspoon white flour and water in small bowl; cover, stand in warm place about 10 minutes or until mixture is frothy.

Sift wholemeal flour and extra white flour into large bowl, stir in yeast mixture and oil, mix to a firm dough. Knead dough on floured surface about 2 minutes or until smooth. Return dough to large greased bowl, cover, stand in warm place about 40 minutes or until dough is doubled in size.

Turn dough onto floured surface, knead until smooth. Divide dough in half, roll each portion into a 23cm round. Place rounds on oven trays, spread with pesto, sprinkle evenly with pepper, mushrooms, artichokes, tomatoes and cheese. Bake in moderately hot oven about 25 minutes or until browned and cooked through. Sprinkle with basil and extra oil. Serve with watercress and witlof salad.
Pesto: Blend or process all ingredients until smooth.

■ Recipe best made just before serving.
■ Freeze: Suitable.
■ Microwave: Not suitable.

WATERCRESS AND WITLOF SALAD

2 small witlof
½ cup firmly packed watercress sprigs

DRESSING
2 teaspoons lemon juice
1 tablespoon olive oil
1 clove garlic, crushed
¼ teaspoon seasoned pepper

Combine separated witlof leaves and watercress in bowl, sprinkle with dressing.
Dressing: Combine all ingredients in jar; shake well.

■ Recipe best made just before serving.
■ Freeze: Not suitable.

Ratatouille and Beans in Pastry Shells

RATATOUILLE AND BEANS IN PASTRY SHELLS

1 sheet ready-rolled puff pastry
1 egg, lightly beaten
1 tablespoon milk

RATATOUILLE
1 tablespoon olive oil
1 small onion, sliced
¼ green pepper, thinly sliced
¼ red pepper, thinly sliced
1 clove garlic, crushed
1 small (about 200g) eggplant, chopped
2 small (about 130g) zucchini, chopped
100g baby mushrooms, halved
¼ cup dry red wine
¼ cup water
2 tablespoons tomato paste
¼ cup pine nuts, toasted
12 black olives, halved
2 tablespoons chopped fresh parsley
2 tablespoons chopped fresh basil
½ cup canned red kidney beans, rinsed, drained
1 medium (about 130g) tomato, peeled, chopped

RED PEPPER SAUCE
2 large red peppers
1 clove garlic, crushed

Grease outside of 2 rounded metal moulds (1 cup capacity). Cut pastry into 2cm strips. Moisten 1 edge of each strip with water.

Wind pastry around moulds, overlapping edges; do not stretch pastry. You will need to join strips of pastry to cover moulds. Brush pastry evenly with combined egg and milk.

Place moulds on oven tray, bake, uncovered, in moderate oven about 15 minutes or until pastry is browned. Remove pastry shells from moulds with small palette knife, cool shells on wire rack. Serve pastry shells filled with hot ratatouille and hot red pepper sauce.

Ratatouille: Heat oil in pan, add onion, peppers and garlic, cook, stirring, until onion is soft. Add eggplant and zucchini, cook, stirring, 3 minutes. Add mushrooms, wine, water, paste, nuts, olives and herbs, cook, stirring, about 5 minutes or until vegetables are just tender. Add beans and tomato, stir until heated through.

Red Pepper Sauce: Quarter peppers, remove seeds and membrane. Grill peppers skin side up until skin blisters and blackens; reserve any juice from peppers. Peel away skin, cool peppers. Blend or process peppers, reserved juice and garlic until smooth.

- ■ Recipe can be made a day ahead.
- ■ Storage: Ratatouille and red pepper sauce, covered, in refrigerator. Pastry shells, in airtight container.
- ■ Freeze: Red pepper sauce suitable.
- ■ Microwave: Ratatouille suitable.

ABOVE: Ratatouille and Beans in Pastry Shells.
LEFT: Pizzas with Pesto and Goats' Cheese and Watercress and Witlof Salad.

DESSERTS

Beautiful to look at and beautiful to eat, our desserts are not complicated. There's a cool and luscious liqueur mousse with caramel oranges, creamy butterscotch bavarois with two sauces, and fruity tortoni using bought ice-cream. Or, hot and luscious are little chocolate and hazelnut steamed puddings. For a lovely texture contrast, try crisp tuiles with light custard cream, on this page. Around half are really easy, such as pears on cinnamon brioche, flambe mangoes, and blueberry puffs with raspberry sauce.

STRAWBERRY AND BANANA TUILES

Use remaining mixture to make more tuiles to serve with coffee or desserts.

1 egg white
¼ cup castor sugar
2 tablespoons plain flour
30g butter, melted
¼ teaspoon coconut essence
1½ tablespoons shredded coconut
4 strawberries
1 small banana

CUSTARD CREAM
⅓ cup milk
1 tablespoon castor sugar
½ teaspoon vanilla essence
2 teaspoons custard powder
2 tablespoons milk, extra
1 egg yolk
¼ cup thickened cream

GLAZE
2 tablespoons strawberry jam
1 tablespoon water

Beat egg white in small bowl with electric mixer until soft peaks form, gradually add sugar, beat until dissolved. Fold in sifted flour, cooled butter and essence. Place 2 level teaspoons of mixture about 5cm apart on 2 greased oven trays. Use back of spoon to spread mixture evenly to about 8cm rounds. Sprinkle with coconut. You will need 4 tuiles for this recipe.

Bake tuiles in moderate oven about 4 minutes or until lightly browned. Lift tuiles from tray with spatula, quickly place 2 tuiles over 2 small upturned moulds; cool. Quickly wrap remaining 2 tuiles around 2 small cream horn moulds; cool.

Fill tuiles with custard cream, top round tuiles with strawberries, top cones with sliced banana. Brush strawberries with a little glaze, drizzle remaining glaze onto serving plates.

Custard Cream: Combine milk, sugar and essence in pan, stir in blended custard powder and extra milk and yolk. Stir over heat until mixture boils and thickens, remove from heat, cover to prevent a skin forming; cool. Beat cream in small bowl until firm peaks form, fold into custard.

Glaze: Combine jam and water in small pan, stir over heat until warm; sieve mixture to remove seeds.

■ Tuiles can be made 2 days ahead.
■ Storage: Airtight container.
■ Freeze: Not suitable.
■ Microwave: Custard and glaze suitable.

RIGHT: Strawberry and Banana Tuiles.

China and glasses from Villeroy & Boch; cloth and serviette from Lillywhites; gift plaque and serviette ring from People's Behaviour.

FROZEN LIQUEUR MOUSSE WITH CARAMEL ORANGES

2 egg yolks
2 teaspoons hot water
1 tablespoon castor sugar
½ cup thickened cream
3 teaspoons Grand Marnier

CARAMEL ORANGES
2 oranges
⅓ cup castor sugar
2 tablespoons water

Line 2 dishes (⅔ cup capacity) with plastic wrap. Beat egg yolks, water and sugar with electric mixer or rotary beater in top of double saucepan over simmering water until thick and creamy. Transfer mixture to small bowl, continue beating with mixer until cool. Beat cream in small bowl until soft peaks form, fold into egg mixture with liqueur. Pour into prepared dishes, cover, freeze until firm. Unmould mousse, serve with caramel oranges.

MACADAMIA TARTLETS

½ cup plain flour
45g butter
1 tablespoon water, approximately

FILLING
1 egg, lightly beaten
¼ cup dark corn syrup or glucose
   syrup
⅓ cup brown sugar
15g butter, melted
½ cup macadamias, coarsely
   chopped

Sift flour into bowl, rub in butter. Add enough water to make ingredients cling together. Press dough into ball, knead gently on lightly floured surface until smooth, cover, refrigerate 30 minutes.

Roll dough on floured surface large enough to line 2 deep 10cm flan tins. Lift pastry into tins gently, ease into sides, trim edges. Place tins on oven tray, line pastry with paper, fill with dried beans or rice. Bake in moderately hot oven 10 minutes, remove paper and beans, bake further 10 minutes or until pastry is browned; cool.

Pour filling into pastry cases, bake in moderately slow oven about 45 minutes or until set; serve warm or cold.

Filling: Combine all ingredients in bowl, mix well.

- Recipe can be made 2 days ahead.
- Storage: Covered, in refrigerator.
- Freeze: Suitable.
- Microwave: Not suitable.

PEARS ON CINNAMON BRIOCHE WITH SPICED CREAM

2 thick slices brioche
20g butter, melted
1 teaspoon ground cinnamon
2 canned drained pear halves
½ teaspoon castor sugar

SPICED CREAM
½ cup thickened cream
1 teaspoon icing sugar
¼ teaspoon ground ginger
½ teaspoon ground cinnamon

Brush brioche on both sides with butter, sprinkle with half the cinnamon. Slice pears, arrange slices over brioche, sprinkle with sugar, place on oven tray. Bake, uncovered, in moderate oven about 20 minutes or until brioche edges are browned and crisp. Sprinkle with remaining cinnamon, serve with spiced cream.

Spiced Cream: Beat cream and sugar in small bowl until firm peaks form, fold in spices gently.

- Brioche best cooked just before serving. Spiced cream can be made 3 hours ahead.
- Storage: Covered, in refrigerator.
- Freeze: Not suitable.
- Microwave: Not suitable.

Caramel Oranges: Peel oranges, cut between membranes into segments, reserve enough juice to make ¼ cup. Combine sugar and water in pan, stir over heat, without boiling, until sugar is dissolved. Boil, uncovered, without stirring, until syrup is honey coloured. Gradually pour in juice, stir until toffee lumps are melted, pour over orange segments; cool.

- Recipe can be prepared 2 days ahead.
- Storage: Mousse, covered, in freezer. Caramel oranges, covered, in refrigerator.
- Freeze: Mousse suitable.
- Microwave: Not suitable.

LEFT: Frozen Liqueur Mousse with Caramel Oranges.
ABOVE: Macadamia Tartlets.
RIGHT: Pears on Cinnamon Brioche with Spiced Cream.

Left: China and glass from Villeroy & Boch.

MANDARINS WITH MANDARIN SABAYON

2 large mandarins
2 egg yolks
2 tablespoons castor sugar
2 teaspoons brandy

Peel mandarins, separate segments, remove seeds, white pith and membrane. Roughly chop three-quarters of the segments; reserve remaining segments.

Blend or process chopped mandarins until smooth; strain, discard pulp. You will need ⅓ cup juice. Combine juice, yolks, sugar and brandy in heatproof bowl. Beat with rotary beater or electric mixer over pan of simmering water about 8 minutes or until thick and foamy.

Divide reserved mandarin segments between 2 glasses, top with mandarin sabayon. Serve immediately.

■ Recipe must be made just before serving.
■ Freeze: Not suitable.
■ Microwave: Not suitable.

APRICOT AND PINEAPPLE TORTONI

This dessert makes about 4 to 6 servings; it will keep, covered, in freezer for 2 weeks.

1 litre vanilla ice-cream, softened
½ x 150g packet coconut macaroons, chopped
4 glace apricots, chopped
2 rings glace pineapple, chopped
1½ tablespoons Grand Marnier or Cointreau
¼ cup slivered almonds, toasted

ALMOND TOFFEE
¼ cup slivered almonds, toasted
½ cup castor sugar
½ cup water

Combine ice-cream, macaroons, fruit, liqueur and nuts in bowl; mix well. Spoon mixture into deep 19cm square cake pan, cover, freeze until firm. Serve tortoni with almond toffee.

Almond Toffee: Spread nuts on greased oven tray. Place sugar and water in pan; stir over heat, without boiling, until sugar is dissolved. Simmer, uncovered, without stirring, about 7 minutes or until syrup is lightly coloured and will crack when a teaspoon of the syrup is dropped into a cup of cold water. Pour over nuts; leave to set. Break into pieces when set.

■ Tortoni and almond toffee can be made 2 days ahead.
■ Storage: Tortoni, covered, in freezer. Almond toffee, in airtight container.
■ Microwave: Not suitable.

LEFT: Mandarins with Mandarin Sabayon.
ABOVE: Apricot and Pineapple Tortoni.

Above: Glassware from Kenwick Galleries.

FLAMBE MANGOES

30g butter
1 tablespoon castor sugar
½ cup orange juice
2 mangoes, sliced
2 tablespoons Cointreau or
 Grand Marnier

Heat butter in pan, add sugar and juice, stir over heat, without boiling, until sugar is dissolved. Simmer, uncovered, without stirring, until syrup just begins to change colour. Add mangoes and liqueur; ignite. Serve immediately with sliced oranges, if desired.

■ Recipe best made just before serving.
■ Freeze: Not suitable.
■ Microwave: Not suitable.

RIGHT: Flambe Mangoes.
BELOW: Poached Fruit with Mascarpone Cheese.

Right: China from Wedgwood. Below: China from Noritake.

POACHED FRUIT WITH MASCARPONE CHEESE

2 small pears
4 fresh dates
2 tamarillos
½ cup water
½ cup dry white wine
¼ cup castor sugar
1 cinnamon stick
1 tablespoon marsala
1 tablespoon marsala, extra
½ cup (120g) mascarpone cheese

Halve pears, leaving stems intact; remove cores. Remove seeds from dates. Make a small slit in skin of tamarillos. Place tamarillos in bowl, cover with boiling water, stand 5 minutes. Remove tamarillos from water; cool, remove skins leaving stems intact.

Combine water, wine and sugar in pan, stir over heat, without boiling, until sugar is dissolved. Add cinnamon and marsala, bring to boil, add pears, cut side down. Simmer gently, covered, about 15 minutes or until pears are tender. Add dates and tamarillos, simmer, covered, further 2 minutes. Remove fruit carefully to serving plates, discard cinnamon.

Simmer remaining sugar syrup, uncovered, until thickened slightly; stir in extra marsala. Spoon syrup over fruit, serve warm or cold with cheese.

■ Recipe can be prepared a day ahead.
■ Storage: Covered, in refrigerator.
■ Freeze: Not suitable.
■ Microwave: Poached fruit suitable.

BLUEBERRY PUFFS
WITH RASPBERRY SAUCE

1 sheet ready-rolled puff pastry
½ cup thickened cream
1 tablespoon icing sugar
**2 teaspoons Grand Marnier or
  Cointreau**
½ punnet (100g) fresh blueberries
1 teaspoon icing sugar, extra

RASPBERRY SAUCE
**1 cup (100g) fresh or frozen
  raspberries**
1 tablespoon icing sugar
**2 tablespoons Grand Marnier or
  Cointreau**

Cut 4 x 11cm rounds from pastry sheet,
place on oven tray. Bake in hot oven
about 10 minutes or until puffed and
browned; cool on wire rack.

Beat cream, icing sugar and liqueur in
small bowl with electric mixer until firm
peaks form. Stir in blueberries. Sandwich
puffs with blueberry cream, dust with extra
sifted icing sugar. If desired, heat a metal
skewer, score puffs with hot skewer.
Serve with raspberry sauce.

Raspberry Sauce: Blend or process berries, icing sugar and liqueur until smooth;
strain through fine sieve, discard seeds.

- Recipe can be prepared 2 hours
  ahead.
- Storage: Puffs, in airtight container.
  Blueberry cream and raspberry
  sauce, covered, in refrigerator.
- Freeze: Not suitable.
- Microwave: Not suitable.

BUTTERSCOTCH BAVAROIS
WITH COFFEE SAUCES

⅓ cup sweetened condensed milk
1 tablespoon golden syrup
2 eggs, separated
⅓ cup cream
1 teaspoon gelatine
2 teaspoons water

COFFEE SAUCES
1 teaspoon dry instant coffee
¼ cup water
1 tablespoon sugar
1 teaspoon cornflour
2 teaspoons water, extra
1 tablespoon cream
3 teaspoons Tia Maria or Kahlua

Lightly oil 2 moulds (1 cup capacity).
Combine condensed milk and golden
syrup in pan, stir over low heat about 3
minutes or until mixture is just changed in
colour; cool 5 minutes. Stir in egg yolks
and cream. Sprinkle gelatine over water in
cup, stand in pan of simmering water, stir
until gelatine is dissolved; cool slightly.

Stir gelatine mixture into caramel mixture, cover, refrigerate about 10 minutes
or until cool and slightly thickened. Beat
egg whites in small bowl with electric

CHOCOLATE HAZELNUT PUDDINGS

50g butter
⅓ cup brown sugar
1 egg
½ cup self-raising flour
3 teaspoons cocoa
2 tablespoons milk
2 tablespoons chopped roasted hazelnuts

VANILLA SAUCE
1 tablespoon castor sugar
1 egg yolk
½ cup cream
½ teaspoon vanilla essence

Grease 2 heatproof moulds (1 cup capacity), dust with flour, shake away excess flour.

Cream butter, sugar and egg in small bowl with electric mixer until light and fluffy. Stir in sifted flour and cocoa with milk; stir in nuts. Spread mixture into prepared moulds, cover loosely with greased rounds of paper, secure with string. Place moulds in pan with enough boiling water to come halfway up sides of moulds; boil, covered, about 30 minutes or until puddings are firm. Turn puddings out, serve hot with vanilla sauce.
Vanilla Sauce: Beat sugar and yolk in small bowl with electric mixer until creamy, add to cream in small pan, stir over low heat until mixture thickens slightly; do not boil. Remove from heat, stir in essence.

- Recipe best made just before serving.
- Freeze: Not suitable.
- Microwave: Suitable.

mixer until soft peaks form, fold into caramel mixture in 2 batches. Pour mixture into prepared moulds, cover, refrigerate several hours or overnight until set.

Turn bavarois onto serving plates, serve with warm coffee sauces. Drop small dots of a little extra cream from tip of teaspoon, pull skewer through dots to form hearts.
Coffee Sauces: Combine coffee, water and sugar in pan, stir over heat, without boiling, until sugar is dissolved. Stir in blended cornflour and extra water, stir over heat until mixture boils and thickens. Divide sauce in half, stir cream into half the mixture and liqueur into the other half.

- Recipe can be made a day ahead.
- Storage: Covered, in refrigerator.
- Freeze: Not suitable.
- Microwave: Gelatine and coffee sauces suitable.

LEFT: Blueberry Puffs with Raspberry Sauce.
ABOVE: Butterscotch Bavarois with Coffee Sauces.
RIGHT: Chocolate Hazelnut Puddings.

Left: China from Noritake. Right: China from Villeroy and Boch; napery from Lillywhites.

GLOSSARY

Here are some terms, names and alternatives to help everyone use and understand our recipes perfectly.

ALMONDS:
Flaked: sliced almonds.
Ground: we used packaged commercially ground nuts.
Slivered: almonds cut lengthways.
AMARETTI BISCUITS: small Italian-style almond macaroons.
BACON RASHERS: bacon slices.
BEEF:
Chuck steak: a forequarter cut.
Eye-fillet: tenderloin.
Minced beef: ground beef.
Scotch fillet: eye of the rib roast; rib-eye roll; cube roll.
Sirloin: steak with or without T-bone; New York-style steak.
Spare ribs: located on the rib end of the belly. Australian spare ribs have some fat and meat; American-style spare ribs are bones with a small amount of meat.
BEETROOT: regular round beet.
BLACK BEAN SAUCE: made from fermented whole and crushed soy beans, water and wheat flour.
BOK CHOY: Chinese chard. Use leaves and young tender parts of stems.
BREADCRUMBS:
Packaged: fine packaged crumbs.
Stale: 2 day old bread crumbed by grating, blending or processing.
BRIOCHE: a yeasted cake-type loaf flavoured with butter and eggs.
BUTTER: use salted or unsalted (sweet) butter; 125g is equal to 1 stick butter.
CABANOSSI: a type of ready-to-eat sausage; also known as cabana.
CALVADOS: apple-flavoured brandy.
CANNELLINI BEANS: butter beans
CARAMBOLA: star fruit.
CHEESE:
Blue vein: semi-soft cheese with fine blue green veins of mould.
Cream: also known as Philly.
Mascarpone: a fresh, unripened, smooth, triple cream cheese.
Parmesan: sharp-tasting cheese. We use fresh cheese, although it is available finely grated.
Ricotta: a fresh, light curd cheese.
Tasty: use a firm, good-tasting cheddar.
CHICK PEAS: garbanzos.
CHILLIES: Small chillies (birds' eye or bird peppers) are the hottest.
Flakes, dried: available at Asian stores.
Powder: the Asian variety is the hottest and is made from ground chillies. It can be used as a substitute for fresh chillies in the proportion of ½ teaspoon ground chilli powder to 1 medium chopped chilli.
CHILLI SAUCE: we used a hot Chinese variety. It consists of chillies, salt and vinegar. We use it sparingly so you can increase amounts in recipes, if desired.
CHOC MELTS: are discs of dark compounded chocolate; ideal for melting and moulding.
CHOY SUM: Chinese broccoli.
CINNAMON STICK: dried inner bark of the shoots of the cinnamon tree.
COCONUT: desiccated coconut.
Flaked: flaked coconut flesh.
Shredded: thin strips of dried coconut.
Cream: available in cans and cartons.
Macaroons: small biscuits (cookies) based on coconut.
COINTREAU: orange-flavoured liqueur.
CORIANDER: also known as cilantro and Chinese parsley. Its seeds are the main ingredient of curry powder.
CORNFLOUR: cornstarch.
CORNMEAL: see polenta.
CORN SYRUP: an imported product; it is available in light or dark colour; either can be substituted for the other.
COUSCOUS: a fine semolina cereal.
CREAM: light pouring cream, also known as half 'n' half.
Sour: a thick commercially cultured soured cream.
Thickened (whipping): double cream or cream with more than 35 percent fat can be used.
CREME DE CASSIS: a blackcurrant-flavoured liqueur.
EGGPLANT: aubergine.
ESSENCE: extract.
FISH SAUCE: made from liquid from salted, fermented anchovies. Has a strong smell and taste; use sparingly.
FILLO PASTRY: tissue-thin pastry bought chilled or frozen.
FIVE SPICE POWDER: a pungent mixture of ground spices which includes cinnamon, cloves, fennel, star anise and Szechwan peppers.
FLOUR:
White plain: all-purpose flour.
White self-raising: substitute plain (all-purpose) flour and baking powder in the proportions of ¾ metric cup plain flour to 2 metric teaspoons baking powder. Sift together several times before using. If using 8oz measuring cup, use 1 cup plain flour to 2 teaspoons baking powder.
Wholemeal plain: wholewheat all-purpose flour.
Wholemeal self-raising: wholewheat self-raising flour; add baking powder to wholemeal plain (all-purpose) flour as above to make wholemeal self-raising flour.
GARAM MASALA: varied combinations of cardamom, cinnamon, cloves, coriander, cumin and nutmeg.
GELATINE: a setting agent. We use powdered gelatine in our recipes.
GHERKIN: cornichon.
GINGER:
Fresh, green or root: scrape away outside skin and grate before using.
Japanese pickled pink: rose pink to red vinegared ginger in thin shavings.
GLUCOSE SYRUP (liquid glucose): is clear with a consistency like honey; it is made from wheat starch.
GOLDEN SYRUP: maple, pancake syrup or honey can be substituted.
GOW GEES PASTRY: wonton wrappers, spring roll or egg pastry sheets can be substituted.
GRAND MARNIER: an orange-flavoured liqueur.

GREEN GINGER WINE: an Australian-made alcoholic sweet wine infused with finely ground ginger.
GREEN PEPPERCORNS: available in cans or jars, pickled in brine.
GREEN SHALLOTS: also known as scallions and spring onions.
HERBS: we have specified when to use fresh or dried herbs. We used dried (not ground) herbs in the proportion of 1:4 for fresh herbs; eg, 1 teaspoon dried herbs instead of 4 teaspoons (1 tablespoon) chopped fresh herbs.
HOI SIN SAUCE: thick sweet Chinese barbecue sauce made from a mixture of salted black beans, onion and garlic.
HORSERADISH CREAM: paste of horseradish, oil, mustard and flavourings.
HUMMUS: paste of chick peas, tahini, garlic, lemon juice and olive oil.
KAHLUA: a coffee-flavoured liqueur.
KUMARA: orange sweet potato.
LAMB:
Cutlet: small, tender rib chop.
Fillet: tenderloin.
Loin: row of chops from mid-section.
Rack: row of cutlets.
Shank: portion of front or back leg with bone in.
LEEK: a member of the onion family; resembles the green shallot but is much larger.
LEMON GRASS: available from Asian food stores and needs to be bruised or chopped before using. It will keep in a jug of water at room temperature for several weeks; the water must be changed daily. It can be bought dried. To reconstitute, place several pieces of dried lemon grass in a bowl; cover with hot water, stand 20 minutes; drain. This amount is a substitute for 1 stem of fresh lemon grass.
LENTILS: require overnight soaking or long cooking except for red lentils.
MIXED SPICE: a blend of ground cinnamon, allspice and nutmeg.
MUSHROOMS:
Baby: small, unopened mushrooms.
Oyster: pale, grey-white mushrooms.
MUSTARD, SEEDED: a French-style mustard with crushed mustard seeds.
NASHI: fruit flavoured like a pear with the crispness of an apple.
NOODLES:
Dried Japanese: fine noodles made from wheat flour, salt and water.
Fresh egg: made from wheat flour and eggs; varying in thickness.
OIL: polyunsaturated vegetable oil.
Olive: virgin oil is obtained only from the pulp of high-grade fruit. Pure olive oil is pressed from the pulp and kernels of second grade olives. Extra virgin olive oil is the purest quality virgin oil.
ONION:
Red Spanish: purplish-red onion with mild flavour.
Spring: vegetables with small white bulbs and long green leaves.
OYSTER SAUCE: a rich brown sauce made from oysters cooked in salt and soy sauce, then thickened with starches.

PARSLEY, FLAT-LEAFED: also known as continental or Italian parsley.
PEAS:
Snow: also known as mange tout (eat all), sugar peas or Chinese peas.
Sugar snap: are small pods with small formed peas inside.
PEPPER, SEASONED: a combination of pepper, red pepper, garlic flakes, paprika and natural chicken extract.
PEPPERS: capsicum or bell peppers.
PIMIENTOS: canned or bottled peppers.
PITA POCKET: 2-layered flat bread, can be cut open to form a pocket.
PLUM SAUCE: a dipping sauce made from plums, sugar, chillies and spices.
POLENTA: usually made from ground corn (maize); similar to cornmeal but coarser and darker in colour. One can be substituted for the other but results will be slightly different.
PORK:
Butterfly: skinless, boneless, mid-loin chop split in half and flattened.
Spare ribs: see Beef spare ribs.
POTATO, CHAT: baby new potato.
PRAWNS: also known as shrimp.
PROSCIUTTO: uncooked, unsmoked ready- to-eat ham cured in salt.
PRUNES: whole dried plums.
PUFF PASTRY, READY-ROLLED: frozen sheets of puff pastry.
PUNNET: small basket usually holding about 250g fruit.
QUAIL: small game birds weighing from about 250g to 300g.
RAVIOLI: small filled pasta.
RICE:
Arborio: large round-grained rice especially suitable for risotto.
Brown: natural whole grain.
Jasmine: fragrant long-grained rice.
White: is hulled and polished, can be short or long grained.
Wild: from North America, but is not a member of the rice family.
RIND: zest.

RISONI: rice-sized, rice-shaped pasta.
SAFFRON: available in strands or ground; the quality varies greatly.
SAKE: Japan's favourite rice wine.
SAMBAL OELEK: (also ulek and olek) a paste made from chillies and salt; can be an ingredient or an accompaniment.
SESAME OIL: made from roasted, crushed white sesame seeds. Do not use for frying.
SHRIMP SAUCE: salted shrimps made into a sauce; has a strong flavour.
SOY SAUCE: made from fermented soy beans. The light sauce is generally used with white meat, and the darker variety with red meat. There is a multi-purpose salt-reduced sauce available, also Japanese soy sauce.
SPATCHCOCK: small chicken weighing about 400g to 500g.
SPINACH, ENGLISH: a soft-leaved vegetable, more delicate in taste than silverbeet (spinach); young silverbeet can be substituted for English spinach.
SPINACH (silverbeet): cook green leafy parts as required by recipes.
STOCK: 1 cup stock is the equivalent of 1 cup water plus 1 crumbled stock cube (or 1 teaspoon stock powder). If you prefer to make your own fresh stock, see recipes in section below.
SUGAR: we used coarse granulated table sugar, also known as crystal sugar, unless otherwise specified.
Brown: a soft fine granulated sugar with molasses present.
Castor: fine granulated table sugar.
SULTANAS: seedless white raisins.
SWEETENED CONDENSED MILK: we use canned milk from which 60 percent of the water has been removed; the remaining milk is then sweetened.
TABASCO SAUCE: made with vinegar, hot red peppers and salt; use sparingly.
TAHINI PASTE: made from crushed sesame seeds.
TAMARILLO: oval fruit with burgundy or yellow skin; has red flesh and tangy flavoured seeds.
TOBLERONE CHOCOLATE: honey and

almond nougat bar.
TOFU: made from boiled, crushed soy beans to give a type of milk. A coagulant is added, much like the process of cheese making. We used firm tofu in this book.
TOMATO:
Cherry tomato: tom thumb tomato.
Paste: a dense tomato puree used in flavouring soups, stews, sauces, etc.
Puree: canned, pureed tomatoes (not tomato paste).
Sun-dried: are dried tomatoes sometimes bottled in oil.
VEAL:
Chops: cut from the rib and loin.
Mince: ground veal.
Rack: row of small chops or cutlets.
Schnitzel: thinly sliced steak.
VINEGAR: we used both white and brown (malt) vinegar in this book.
Balsamic: regional wine is specially processed then aged in antique wooden casks to give a pungent flavour.
Cider: made from apples.
Raspberry: made from raspberries steeped in white wine vinegar.
Rice: a colourless seasoned vinegar containing sugar and salt.
Tarragon: fresh tarragon is infused in white wine vinegar.
Wine: made from wine, often flavoured with herbs, spices, fruit, etc.
VOL-AU-VENT CASE: flaky pastry case ready for filling.
WASABI PASTE OR POWDER: green horseradish.
WITLOF: also known as chicory or Belgian endive.
WONTON WRAPPERS: see gow gees.
YEAST: allow 2 teaspoons (7g) dried yeast to each 15g compressed yeast if substituting one for the other.
ZUCCHINI: courgette.

MAKE YOUR OWN STOCK

BEEF STOCK

2kg meaty beef bones
2 onions
2 sticks celery, chopped
2 carrots, chopped
3 bay leaves
2 teaspoons black peppercorns
5 litres (20 cups) water
3 litres (12 cups) water, extra

Place bones and unpeeled chopped onions in baking dish. Bake, uncovered, in hot oven about 1 hour or until bones and onions are well browned. Transfer bones and onions to large pan, add celery, carrots, bay leaves, peppercorns and water, simmer, uncovered, 3 hours. Add extra water, simmer, uncovered, further 1 hour; strain.
Makes about 10 cups.
- ■ Stock can be made 4 days ahead.
- ■ Storage: Covered, in refrigerator.
- ■ Freeze: Suitable.
- ■ Microwave: Not suitable.

CHICKEN STOCK

2kg chicken bones
2 onions, chopped
2 sticks celery, chopped
2 carrots, chopped
3 bay leaves
2 teaspoons black peppercorns
5 litres (20 cups) water

Combine all ingredients in large pan, simmer, uncovered, 2 hours; strain.
Makes about 10 cups.
- ■ Stock can be made 4 days ahead.
- ■ Storage: Covered, in refrigerator.
- ■ Freeze: Suitable.
- ■ Microwave: Not suitable.

FISH STOCK

1½kg fish bones
3 litres (12 cups) water
1 onion, chopped
2 sticks celery, chopped
2 bay leaves
1 teaspoon black peppercorns

Combine all ingredients in large pan, simmer, uncovered, 20 minutes; strain.
Makes about 10 cups.
- ■ Stock can be made 4 days ahead.
- ■ Storage: Covered, in refrigerator.
- ■ Freeze: Suitable.
- ■ Microwave: Not suitable.

VEGETABLE STOCK

1 large carrot, chopped
1 large parsnip, chopped
2 onions, chopped
6 sticks celery, chopped
4 bay leaves
2 teaspoons black peppercorns
3 litres (12 cups) water

Combine all ingredients in large pan, simmer, uncovered, 1½ hours; strain.
Makes about 5 cups.
- ■ Stock can be made 4 days ahead.
- ■ Storage: Covered, in refrigerator.
- ■ Freeze: Suitable.
- ■ Microwave: Not suitable.

INDEX

Cup and Spoon Measurements

To ensure accuracy in your recipes use the standard metric measuring equipment approved by Standards Australia:

(a) 250 millilitre cup for measuring liquids. A litre jug *(capacity 4 cups)* is also available.

(b) a graduated set of four cups – measuring 1 cup, half, third and quarter cup – for items such as flour, sugar, etc. When measuring in these fractional cups, level off at the brim.

(c) a graduated set of four spoons: tablespoon *(20 millilitre liquid capacity)*, teaspoon *(5 millilitre)*, half and quarter teaspoons. The Australian, British and American teaspoon each has 5ml capacity.

Approximate cup and spoon conversion chart

Australian	American & British
1 cup	1¼ cups
¾ cup	1 cup
⅔ cup	¾ cup
½ cup	⅔ cup
⅓ cup	½ cup
¼ cup	⅓ cup
2 tablespoons	¼ cup
1 tablespoon	4 teaspoons

ALL SPOON MEASUREMENTS ARE LEVEL.
Note: *NZ, Canada, USA and UK all use 15ml tablespoons.*

Oven Temperatures

Electric	C°	F°
Very slow	120	250
Slow	150	300
Moderately slow	160-180	325-350
Moderate	180-200	375-400
Moderately hot	210-230	425-450
Hot	240-250	475-500
Very hot	260	525-550

Gas	C°	F°
Very slow	120	250
Slow	150	300
Moderately slow	160	325
Moderate	180	350
Moderately hot	190	375
Hot	200	400
Very hot	230	450

We have used large eggs with an average weight of 60g each in all recipes.

TWO GREAT OFFERS FROM THE AWW HOME LIBRARY